Canada
Provinces and Territories

—— Grades 4-6 ——

Written by Ruth Solski
Revised January 2016

Canadian children should be exposed to and become more knowledgeable with their wonderful country. This book has been written to acquaint and to expand student knowledge of Canada's Physical Regions, Climate, Provinces, Territories, Capital Cities, Bodies of Water, Natural Resources, Industrial Growth, and its People. During this study, students will develop and strengthen reading, research, and mapping skills.

RUTH SOLSKI was an educator for 30 years. She has written many educational resources and is the founder of S&S Learning Materials. As a writer, her main goal is to provide teachers with a useful tool that they can implement in their classrooms to bring the joy of learning to children.

Published in Canada by:
On The Mark Press
15 Dairy Avenue, Napanee, Ontario, K7R 1M4
www.onthemarkpress.com

Funded by the Government of Canada
Financé par le gouvernement du Canada

Canada

 # CANADA'S PROVINCES AND TERRITORIES

Table of Contents

 # CANADA'S PROVINCES AND TERRITORIES

Learning Expectations

Students will:

• describe the physical features of regions within the provinces.

• identify how regions are interdependent in relation to their economies and governments.

• demonstrate and become aware of the various relationships, economically and culturally, etc., within and between Canadian regions.

• identify the characteristics of the physical regions of their individual province/territory and all of Canada.

• name and describe the main features of a river system.

• demonstrate an understanding of the significance of the St. Lawrence River and the Great Lakes System.

• identify Canada's major natural resources and their uses.

• identify and describe types of communities in each physical region of each province and territory.

• demonstrate an understanding of the exchange of products within each province or territory and throughout Canada.

• identify the physical regions of Canada.

• describe and compare the physical environments of these regions according to land forms.

• identify the natural resources used to create Canadian products and the provinces/territories from which they originate.

• use appropriate vocabulary to describe their inquiries and observations.

• construct and read a variety of graphs, charts, diagrams, maps, and models for specific purposes such as to determine physical features, area of regions, size of populations, climate, etc.

• identify Ottawa as the capital city of Canada.

• locate and label the Great Lakes and other major bodies of water and waterways in Canada.

• identify symbols used to outline boundaries (international, national, provincial).

• locate and label the physical regions of Canada on a map.

• use cardinal and intermediate directions, non-pictorial symbols, and colour on a map to locate and describe physical regions.

CANADA'S PROVINCES AND TERRITORIES

Teacher Input Suggestions

1. **Planning Ahead:**

   Locate any of the following items.

   Canadian atlases; reference books on Canada; reference books on the individual provinces and territories; travel brochures and pamphlets on the various provinces/territories; travel posters about Canada and Canadian places; large photographs or picture collections on places located in the provinces and territories; road maps of the various provinces and territories; wall maps of the world, North America, Canada; photos of tourist attractions across Canada; photos of different types of communities found in Canada; photographs of ethnic people to show the students that Canada is a multi-cultural nation; photos of provincial and territorial coat of arms, flags, floral emblems, animals, birds; postcards of different places located in Canada; photos of Canada's capital city, government buildings, and the present Prime Minister of Canada; puzzles of Canadian scenes and maps of Canada.

2. **Introduction:**

   - Decorate your classroom door with Canadian flags, maple leaves, and a large sign that says "**WELCOME TO CANADA!**" On either side of the door, display a full size picture of an R.C.M.P. officer standing guard. On the inside of the door, display labelled pictures of Canada, copies of Canadian songs, and poetry.

   - Play Canada's National Anthem, "O Canada," and sing the words. On a chart or white board, display the words and discuss what they mean. Teach your own provincial/territorial song if there is one.

   - Show a film or video that provides an overview of Canada from coast to coast. Discuss it with your students. Show a film or video on your own province/territory if possible.

   - Brainstorm with your students for facts that they already know about Canada. List the facts on the chalkboard, white board, or on a chart. This could also be done by dividing the class into different groups. Provide each group with a marker and chart paper. Each group has a leader and a recorder. The leader selects students with facts and the recorder records them on the chart.

   - Brainstorm with your students for questions that they would like answered about Canada or their own province. This could also be done using the same format as the exercise above. Remind the leader of each group to leave a space below each question for the answer to be recorded.

3. **Bulletin Board Displays:**

   - Locate a large map of Canada. Display it on a bulletin board. Pin one end of a piece of string to each province or territory. Attach the other end to the bulletin board outside the map area. Make name cards for all the provinces and territories. Store the name cards in an envelope close to the map. Have the students practise naming them by pinning the name card at the end of each piece of string.

   - Laminate a large, empty, political map that shows the divisions and borders of the various

provinces and territories. This map should also show the position of each capital city. The students may use a water-soluable pen to mark on the names of the provinces and territories and their capital cities. Provide a damp cloth to remove the names after each group of students has identified the different provinces, territories, and their capital cities.

- Display pictures of famous tourist attractions around a large map of Canada. Connect each picture with string to its location in Canada. The pictures should be labelled.

- Around a large map, display pictures of various communities found in Canada. Use large paper arrows to show where the communities are located.

4. **White Board Displays:** Many of the above bulletin board displays could be done using a white board.

5. **Music Ideas:**

   - Teach your class songs that pertain to Canada and the different provinces.

   - Listen to Canadian folk music and popular music sung by professional Canadian artists.

   - Incorporate ethnic music during the theme to familiarize students with multicultural music.

6. **Art Ideas:**

   - Students may paint a mural to show different types of communities located in Canada.

   - Individual pictures of places in Canada, tourist attractions, flags, coats of arms, and floral emblems could be painted, crayoned, or chalked.

   - Collages may be made using photos of different parts of Canada.

   - Post cards and tourist brochures could be designed advertising different tourist attractions in Canada.

7. **Creative Writing Ideas:**

   - Students could source out a Canadian pen pal living in a different province/territory, and begin writing to him or her. The students would tell them facts about their province or territory and ask them questions about theirs. Letters could be read aloud in class.

   - A classroom in one province could communicate using a computer with other classes in different provinces or territories to find out facts and information.

   - Students could read different Canadian legends and then rewrite one to make a storybook for younger students to listen to or read.

   - Adventure stories could be created about different places located in Canada.

   - Descriptive stories could be written about unique places in Canada. For example: Niagara Falls, Rocky Mountains, Whistler, Royal Tyrell Museum, Casa Loma, CN Tower, Fort Henry, Black Creek Pioneer Village, etc.

8. **Organization of this Book:**
   This book has been divided into lesson plans with reproducible follow-ups. Each lesson may need to be adapted or the ideas may be used to design you own lesson plans in order to suit the needs of your own students.

 CANADA'S PROVINCES AND TERRITORIES

Lesson Plan #1: Where is Canada?

Expectations:

The students will:

- identify, locate, and label the continents and the oceans of the world.
- identify Canada's location in the world.
- recall and record learned information.

Discussion Time:

1. Using a wall map or a globe, explain to the students that the world is made up of large land masses and large bodies of water. The land masses are divided into seven continents and the water is divided into four oceans. Locate the continents one at a time on the map of the world or on a globe. Discuss their size, shape, location, and the countries involved with each one.

2. Record the name of each continent on a chart or the chalkboard. Beside each one, record its size in square kilometres.

   * Asia - 44 008 000 sq. km.
   * North America - 24 211 000 sq. km.
   * Antarctica - 14 000 000 sq. km.
   * Australia - 7 713 000 sq. km.
   * Africa - 30 253 000 sq. km.
   * South America - 17 833 000 sq. km.
   * Europe - 10 445 000 sq. km.

   Star the continent that is the largest. The continents may then be numbered according to size from the largest to the smallest.

3. Locate the various oceans. Record their names on a chart or chalkboard. Beside each one, record its size.

   * Pacific Ocean - 168 723 000 sq. km.
   * Indian Ocean - 70 560 000 sq. km.
   * Southern Ocean - 21 960 000 sq. km.
   * Atlantic Ocean - 85 133 000 sq. km.
   * Arctic Ocean - 15 558 000 sq. km.

4. Have the students locate Canada on a world wall map. Discuss the continent in which Canada is found. What are the names of the two other countries found in the same continent? (United States, Mexico)

Follow-Ups:

1. Reproduce Map #1 entitled "**Continents of the World**" on page 7. On the map, the students are to locate and label the seven continents and four oceans. They are also to locate Canada and colour Canada red.

2. Reproduce Worksheet #1 entitled "**Where is Canada**?" on page 8. The students are to complete the sheet by recording the correct answers on the lines.

Answer Key for Map of the World: "Where is Canada?" page 7

Lines: 1. Arctic Ocean 2. Pacific Ocean 3. Atlantic Ocean 4. Indian Ocean 5. Southern Ocean
Boxes: 1. North America 2. South America 3. Europe 4. Africa 5. Asia 6. Australia 7. Antarctica

Worksheet #1: "Where is Canada?" page 8

Order of missing words: second; northern; North America; United States; Mexico; 9 970 610; Russia; A continent is one of the seven dry land masses on the earth.; An ocean is a great body of salt water.; Oceans cover three quarters of the Earth's surface. The seven continents found in the world are: 1. Africa 2. Asia 3. Antarctica 4. Australia 5. Europe 6. North America 7. South America; The five oceans found in the world are 1. Arctic Ocean 2. Atlantic Ocean 3. Pacific Ocean 4. Indian Ocean 5. Southern Ocean

Map of the World: Where is Canada?

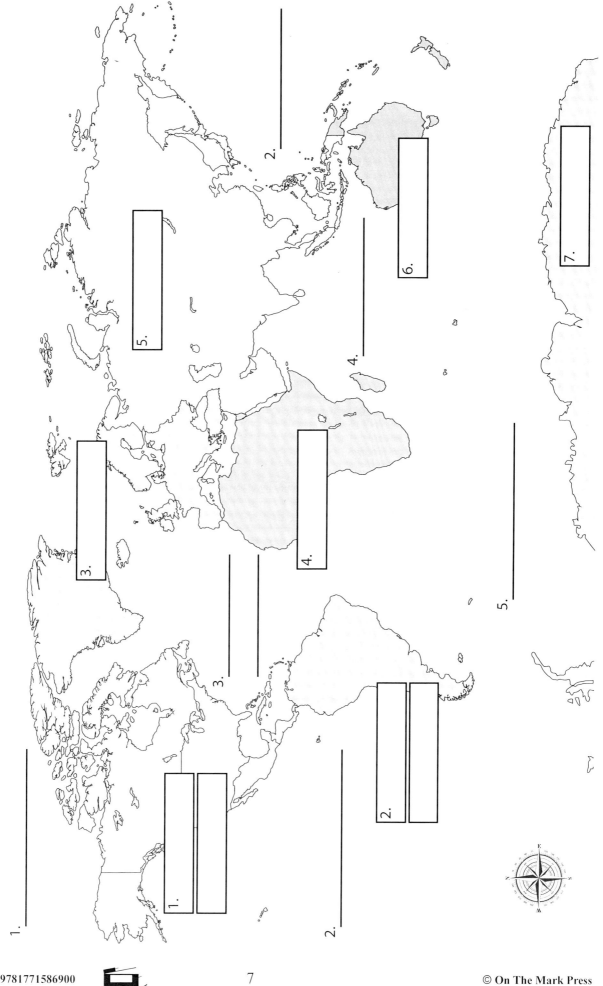

SSJ192   ISBN 9781771586900

CANADA'S PROVINCES AND TERRITORIES

Worksheet #1: Where is Canada?

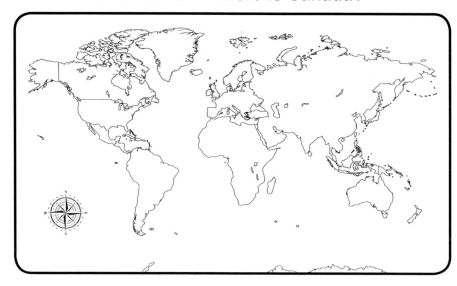

Canada is the _____ largest country in the world. It covers the

_____ half of the continent called _____ except for

Alaska. It shares this continent with the _____ and _____.

Canada is _____ sq.km. in area. There is only one country that is larger than

Canada. It is called _____.

What is a continent?:

_____

_____

What is an ocean?:

_____

_____

The seven continents found in the world are:

1._____   5._____

2._____   6._____

3._____   7._____

4._____

The five oceans found in the world are:

1._____   4._____

2._____   5._____

3._____

 CANADA'S PROVINCES AND TERRITORIES

Lesson Plan #2: Canada's Borders

Expectations:

The student will

- identify Canada's borders within the country.
- identify and label Canada's borders with another country.
- recall and record learned information.

Discussion Time:

Use a large wall map of Canada or one on a white board to show the country and the bodies of water that border it. Have the students locate the United States and Alaska. Locate the bodies of water that border Canada. They are: Hudson Bay, Arctic Ocean, Atlantic Ocean, Pacific Ocean.

Follow-Ups:

1. Reproduce Worksheet #1 entitled "Canada's Borders" on page 10. On the map, have the students trace in green the border lines of Canada. Print the names of the bodies of water and the country that borders Canada. With a red pencil crayon, the students can then trace the border lines that divide Canada into provinces and territories.

2. **Answer key for Worksheet #1: Canada's Borders** page 10

   A. Map: 1. Arctic Ocean 2. Alaska 3. Pacific Ocean 4. Hudson Bay 5. Atlantic Ocean
   6. The United States

   B. 1. A border is the side, edge, or boundary of anything. It can be a line which separates one
   country, state, or province from another. It can be a coastline.

   2. Pacific Ocean and Alaska

   3. Atlantic Ocean

   4. Arctic Ocean, Hudson Bay

   5. United States

   6. 13

   7. No

   8. 11

   9. 2

CANADA'S PROVINCES AND TERRITORIES

Worksheet #1: Canada's Borders

Part A.

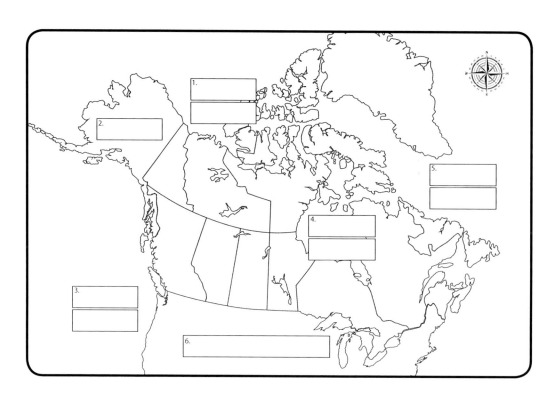

Part B.

1. What is a border? _____

   _____

   _____

   _____

2. In the west, Canada borders on the _____ and _____.

3. In the east, Canada borders on the _____.

4. In the north, Canada borders on the _____ and _____.

5. In the south, Canada borders on the _____.

6. Into how many areas has Canada been divided? _____

7. Are the areas in Canada all the same size? _____

8. How many areas are bordered by water? _____

9. How many areas are bordered by other land areas? _____

Lesson Plan #3: Canada's Provinces and Territories

Expectations:

The students will:

- identify and locate each territory and province found in Canada.
- label each province and territory correctly on a map of Canada.
- identify the provinces called Atlantic Provinces, Prairie Provinces, and the Territories.
- identify their own province or territory.

Discussion Time:

Point to a wall map of Canada or one on a white board and explain that Canada is divided into thirteen different land areas that are called provinces or territories. Pose the following questions. "Who can locate and name the province in which we live?, Can someone find another province or territory and tell us its name?, Once all the provinces and territories are located, have the students identify the provinces by using a compass rose.

Example: Which province is to the west of Ontario? (Manitoba) Which province is east of Alberta? (Saskatchewan)

Follow-ups:

1. Reproduce the map entitled "Canada's Provinces and Territories" located on page 12. Place the same map on an overhead or white board. Working from the Atlantic Coast to the Pacific Coast, have the students name and label each province neatly by printing on the lines in the rectangles provided. Then have the students label the territories. The students will also colour each province and territory a different colour.

2. Reproduce worksheet entitled "Canada's Provinces and Territories" found on page 13. The students will record the answers required on the worksheet.

Answer Key for Map of Canada's Provinces and Territories page 12

1. Newfoundland/Labrador 2. Prince Edward Island 3. Nova Scotia 4. New Brunswick
5. Québec 6. Ontario 7. Manitoba 8. Saskatchewan 9. Alberta 10. British Columbia
11. Yukon 12. Northwest Territories 13. Nunavut

Answer Key for Worksheet #1: Canada's Provinces and Territories page 13

1. ten; territories
2. Alberta, British Columbia, Manitoba, New Brunswick, Newfoundland and Labrador, Northwest Territories, Nova Scotia, Nunavut, Ontario, Prince Edward Island, Québec, Saskatchewan, Yukon Territory
3. Prince Edward Island
4. Nova Scotia, Newfoundland and Labrador, New Brunswick, Prince Edward Island
5. Manitoba, Saskatchewan, Alberta
6. Yukon Territory, Northwest Territories, Nunavut

Canada's Provinces and Territories

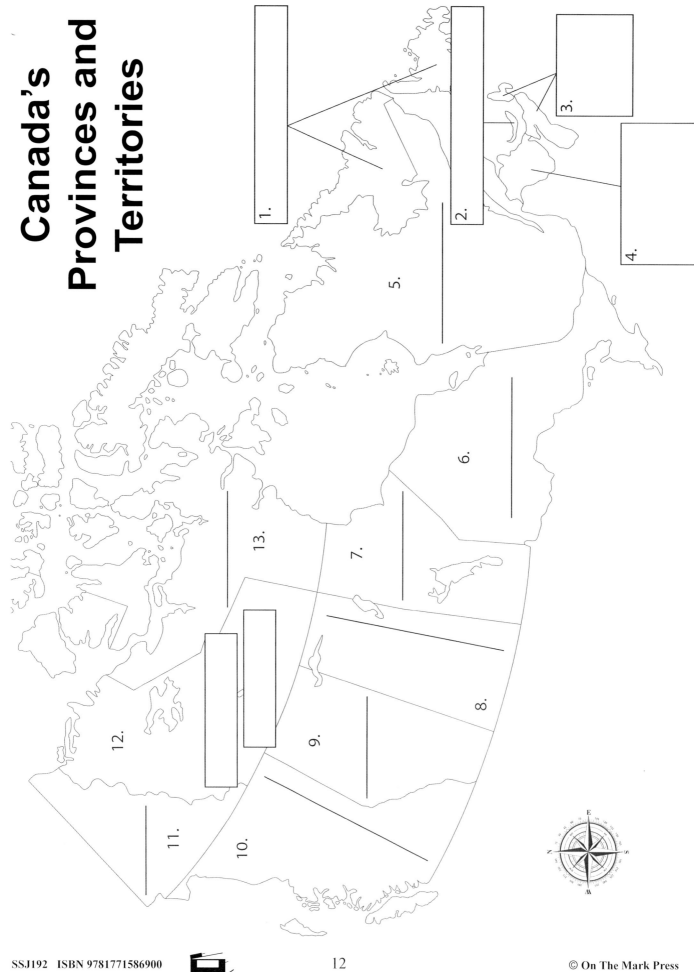

SSJ192   ISBN 9781771586900

 CANADA'S PROVINCES AND TERRITORIES

Worksheet #1: Canada's Provinces and Territories

1. Canada has _____ provinces and three _____.

2. The names of Canada's provinces and territories are listed on the flag.
   Can you write their names in the correct alphabetical order?

Nunavut

Ontario

Alberta

Manitoba

Newfoundland & Labrador

Québec

Nova Scotia

Yukon Territory

Saskatchewan

British Columbia

Northwest Territories

Prince Edward Island

New Brunswick

_____

_____

_____

_____

_____

_____

_____

_____

_____

_____

_____

_____

_____

3. Which province is an island? _____

4. Write the names of the Atlantic Provinces.

_____

_____

5. Write the names of the Prairie Provinces.

_____

_____

6. Write the names of the territories.

_____

_____

SSJ192 ISBN 9781771586900

Lesson Plan #4: Borders Inside Canada

Expectations:

The students will:

- use a map to locate information.
- identify and complete borders between provinces.
- label a political outline map of Canada independently.

Discussion:

The students will use their labelled political map of Canada found on page 12 to locate the answers to the following questions.

1. Which two provinces share the shortest border? (***New Brunswick, Nova Scotia***)

2. Which province has its border entirely surrounded by salt water? (***Prince Edward Island***)

3. Which provinces border on Hudson Bay? (***Manitoba, Ontario, Québec***)

4. Which province borders on the Pacific Ocean? (***British Columbia***)

5. Which province's northern border is found on Nunavut? (***Manitoba***)

6. Which provinces share their southern borders with the United States? Name them from east to west. (***New Brunswick, Québec, Ontario, Manitoba, Saskatchewan, Alberta, British Columbia***)

7. Which territory shares its western border with the Northwest Territories? (***Nunavut***)

8. Which territory shares its borders with Alaska and British Columbia? (***Yukon Territory***)

9. Which province shares its eastern border with Québec and its western border with Manitoba? (***Ontario***)

10. Which province shares its borders with Québec and the Atlantic Ocean? (***Newfoundland and Labrador***)

11. Which two provinces do not have borders on any water? (***Alberta, Saskatchewan***)

12. Which province has borders on fresh water and salt water? (***Ontario***)

13. Which two provinces have the Ottawa River as a border? (***Ontario, Québec***)

Follow-Ups:

1. Reproduce map entitled "Borders Inside Canada" (page 16). Have the students complete the broken borders found on the map. Then have them practise labelling the provinces and territories. This activity could be repeated many times until the students become quite proficient recalling the borders and names of the provinces and territories.

2. Reproduce Worksheet #1 entitled "Border Riddles" (page 17). The students will read the riddle and locate the province or territory on a map, then record its name on the line at the end of the riddle.

3. Reproduce Worksheet #2 entitled "Canada Word Search" (page 18). The students are to locate and circle the names of the provinces in green, the territories in red, and the capital cities in blue.

CANADA'S PROVINCES AND TERRITORIES

Answer Key for Map (Page 16):

Answer Key for Map: Names of Provinces and Territories page 16:
1. Newfoundland and Labrador
2. Prince Edward Island 3. Nova Scotia
4. New Brunswick 5. Quebec 6. Ontario
7. Manitoba 8. Saskatchewan 9. Alberta
10. British Columbia 11. Yukon Territory
12. Northwest Territory 13. Nunavut

Answer Key for Worksheet: Border Riddles page 17
1. British Columbia 2. Nova Scotia
3. Ontario 4. Nunavut 5. New Brunswick
6. The Northwest Territories 7. Alberta
8. Manitoba 9. The Yukon Territory
10. Prince Edward Island
11. Saskatchewan 12. Québec
13. Newfoundland and Labrador

Answer Key for Worksheet: Canada Word Search page 18

```
T M K Q U E B E C C I T Y T U V A N U N P O
E A D S B U W I B J O I F S N G A I N O M A
V N R A Q H C O N T A R I O Z F H B L V C I
F I Q A L U I T G T J R Q E P X E K D A J R
X T G L P Z L T V H C T O R O N T O V S U O
N O O B Y M A A K U L D W Y M Q W A T C Y T
C B S E F W G W H I T E H O R S E X B O Z C
T A Q R P O V A A I B M Y N F S G R C T I I
R D U T E H K J N X L N M Z H L E K J I D V
H C H A R L O T T E T O W N A R W L Y A P S
I G F V E U J T K D S R L E O B X P Z Q M Q
P Y U K O N D X F B Z T A W I N N I P E G R
O E U Q T A W E C Y H H I F O Y E N A A N E
S L V Q V W U G V T J W K O L O W M G N F D
R L P K R E U J H W I E X U Z D B C B I E M
W O S T N H R P L M I S Q N E B R Y W G Z O
Z W I S B C O E N H H T I D V Q U E B E C N
D K A L H T X Q O N G T G L F J N C A R X T
F N M J Y A G C T O T E U A K L S M D U B O
X I T M V K Y R C F D R Q N K Z W T Y N X N
U F K Z L S A N I S R R J D S D I O A C V W
Q E R A O A D M R N P I R T Z G C F H M I N
L Y S B C S E E E N O T K P W X K Q P J O R
A C Z B B C F L D P E O U S F A K K G G S M
B W X T D G K D E J Q R I V Y J I L J L H T
R Y D U A F H B R I T I S H C O L U M B I A
A U E C I E G S F U B E E C D D F W N I N C
D M Z S Q J R R V L A S Q P V E O G H X J O
O V H P D N A L S I D R A W D E E C N I R P
R I J O G W T F U X M L M K V Z R U Y P B T
N H A L I F A X Z X X Y W S T J O H N S A S Q
```

Borders Inside Canada

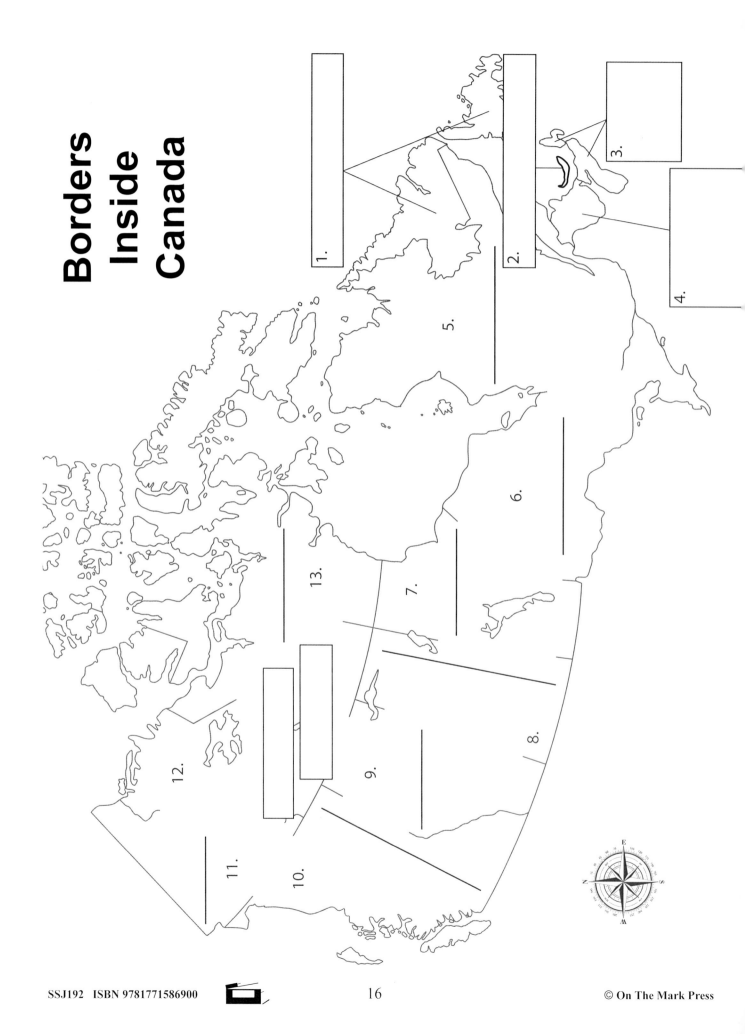

SSJ192   ISBN 9781771586900

CANADA'S PROVINCES AND TERRITORIES

Worksheet #1: Border Riddles

Which Province or Territory Am I?

1. I border the Pacific Ocean on the west, Alberta on the east, the Yukon Territory and Northwest Territories on the north, and the United States on the south.
   I am _____.

2. I have a short land border on the north and a longer border on the Atlantic Ocean.
   I am _____.

3. I border the Great Lakes and the United States on the south, Québec on the east, Manitoba on the west, and Hudson Bay on the north.
   I am _____.

4. I border the Northwest Territories on the west, the Atlantic Ocean on the north and east, and Manitoba on the south.
   I am _____.

5. I border Québec on the north, the United States on the west, the Atlantic Ocean on the east, and the Bay of Fundy on the south.
   I am _____.

6. My eastern border is on Nunavut, my northern border is the Arctic Ocean, and my western border is on the Yukon Territory.
   I am _____.

7. To the north I border the Northwest Territories, to the south I border the United States, on the east I border Saskatchewan, and on the west I border British Columbia.
   I am _____.

8. I border Nunavut on the north, the United States on the south, Ontario on the east, and Saskatchewan on the west.
   I am _____.

9. My western border is the state of Alaska, my eastern border is the Northwest Territories, my northern border is the Arctic Ocean, and my southern border is British Columbia.
   I am _____.

10. My border is the Atlantic Ocean.
    I am _____.

11. I border Alberta on the west, Manitoba on the east, the Northwest Territories on the north, and the United States on the south.
    I am _____.

12. I border Ontario on the west, the United States and New Brunswick on the south, Newfoundland and Labrador on the east, and James Bay, Hudson Bay, and Ungava Bay on the north.
    I am _____.

13. I border Québec on the west and south, and the Atlantic Ocean on the east and all around me.
    I am _____.

Canada's Provinces and Territories

Worksheet #2: Canada Word Search

In the Word Search look for the names of all the provinces, territories, and capital cities found in Canada. Circle the names of the provinces green. Circle the names of the territories red. Circle the names of the capital cities in blue.

```
T M K Q U E B E C C I T Y T U V A N U N P O
E A D S B U W I B J O I F S N G A I N O M A
V N R A Q H C O N T A R I O Z F H B L V C I
F I Q A L U I T G T J R Q E P X E K D A J R
X T G L P Z L T V H C T O R O N T O V S U O
N O O B Y M A A K U L D W Y M Q W A T C Y T
C B S E F W G W H I T E H O R S E X B O Z C
T A Q R P O V A A I B M Y N F S G R C T I I
R D U T E H K J N X L N M Z H L E K J I D V
H C H A R L O T T E T O W N A R W L Y A P S
I G F V E U J T K D S R L E O B X P Z Q M Q
P Y U K O N D X F B Z T A W I N N I P E G R
O E U Q T A W E C Y H H I F O Y E N A A N E
S L V Q V W U G V T J W K O L O W M G N F D
R L P K R E U J H W I E X U Z D B C B I E M
W O S T N H R P L M I S Q N E B R Y W G Z O
Z W I S B C O E N H H T I D V Q U E B E C N
D K A L H T X Q O N G T G L F J N C A R X T
F M N J Y A G C T O T E U A K L S M D U B O
X I T M V K Y R C F D R Q N K Z W T Y N X N
U F K Z L S A N I S R R J D S D I O A C V W
Q E R A O A D M R N P I R T Z G C F H M I N
X Y S B C S E E E N O T K P W X K Q P J O R
W C Z B B C F L D P E O U S F A K K G G S M
W W X T D G K D E H Q R I V Y J I L J L H T
V Y D U A F H B R I T I S H C O L U M B I A
B U E C I E G S F U B E E C D D F W N I N C
K M Z S Q J R R V L A S Q P V E O G H X J O
T V H P D N A L S I D R A W D E E C N I R P
L I J O G W T F U X M L M K V Z R U Y P B T
N H A K I F A X Z X Y W S T J O H N S A S Q
```

CANADA'S PROVINCES AND TERRITORIES

Lesson Plan #5: Canada's Capital Cities

Expectations:

The students will:

- identify and locate each capital city on a map of Canada.
- associate each capital city to its province and territory.
- associate each province and territory to its two-letter designator.

Discussion Time:

A) Using a wall map or a political map of Canada found in an atlas, locate the capital city of each province and territory with your students. Draw attention to the legend or key to find out how a capital city is marked on a map. Work from the east coast to the west coast and then to the north. On the chalkboard or a chart, list the names of the provinces and territories. Beside each one, write the capital city as the students locate it.

Example:

Province	Capital City	Designator

New Brunswick – Fredericton; Québec – Québec City; Ontario – Toronto; Newfoundland & Labrador – St. John's; Prince Edward Island – Charlottetown; Nova Scotia – Halifax; Canada – Ottawa; Manitoba – Winnipeg; Saskatchewan – Regina; Alberta – Edmonton; British Columbia – Victoria; Yukon – Whitehorse; Northwest Territories – Yellowknife; Nunavut – Iqaluit

B) Explain to the students that each province and territory has a provincial capital and the country has a national capital called "Ottawa." Each capital city is the place where the provincial government meets and the national capital is where the federal government meets. Each province also has a two-letter designator. Record the designator on the chart as well. The designator has replaced the abbreviated forms used years ago.

Alberta – AB; British Columbia – BC; Manitoba – MB; New Brunswick – NB; Newfoundland & Labrador – NF; Northwest Territories – NT; Nova Scotia – NS; Nunavut – NU; Ontario – ON; Prince Edward Island – PE; Québec – QC; Saskatchewan – SK; Yukon Territory – YT

Follow-Ups:

1. Reproduce the map entitled "**Canada's Capital Cities**" page 21. Students will record the name of each capital city on the line, and underline the name of the capital city of Canada in red.

2. Reproduce Worksheet entitled **"Let's Research Canada"** page 22. The students will use reference materials to locate the answers to the questions about the provinces, territories, and their capital cities. They will record their findings on the line after each question.

Answer Key for Map: Canada's Capital Cities page 21

1. St. John's 2. Charlottetown 3. Halifax 4. Fredericton 5. Toronto 6. Ottawa 7. Québec City 8. Winnipeg 9. Regina 10. Edmonton 11. Victoria 12. Whitehorse 13. Yellowknife 14. Iqaluit

Answer Key for Worksheet #1: Let's Research Canada page 22

1. Nunavut 2. Québec 3. Prince Edward Island 4. Edmonton 5. Regina, Victoria 6. British Columbia, Alberta 7. Winnipeg 8. Toronto 9. Trillium 10. Northwest Territories 11. Ontario 12. Québec City 13. New Brunswick 14. Prince Edward Island 15. Nova Scotia 16. British Columbia

Canada's Capital Cities

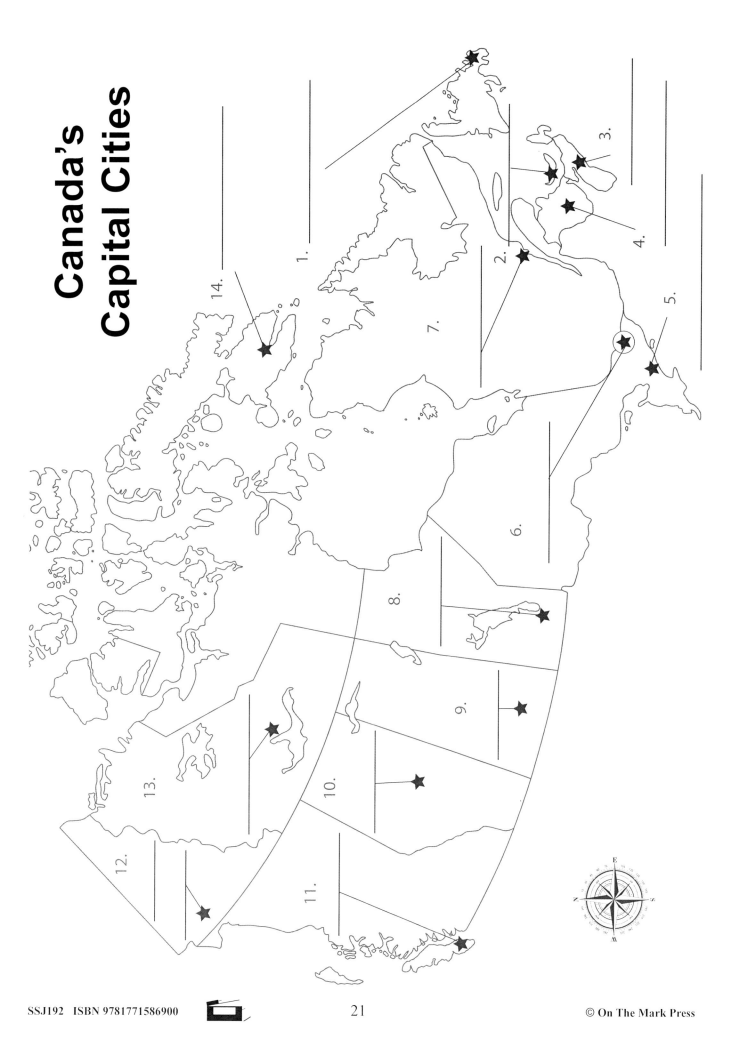

1. _____

2. _____

3. _____

4. _____

5. _____

6. _____

7. _____

8. _____

9. _____

10. _____

11. _____

12. _____

13. _____

14. _____

SSJ192   ISBN 9781771586900

 CANADA'S PROVINCES AND TERRITORIES

Worksheet # 1: Let's Research Canada

1. Which territory in Canada is the largest one?

   _____

2. Which province in Canada is the largest?

   _____

3. Which province is an island connected to Canada by a very long bridge?

   _____

4. In which capital city will you find the largest shopping mall in Canada?

   _____

5. Which two capital cities are named after Queen Victoria?

   _____

6. In which provinces are the Rocky Mountains located?

   _____

7. Which capital city is known as "The Crossroads City?"

   _____

8. Which capital city has the largest population?

   _____

9. What is the floral emblem of Ontario?

   _____

10. Which territory has two very large lakes?

    _____

11. Which province has one of the "Seven Wonders of the World?"

    _____

12. Which capital city is a walled city in Canada?

    _____

13. In which province will you find the flowerpot rocks?

    _____

14. In which province did the heroine of Lucy Maud Montgomery's classic story
    live?   _____

15. in which province would you find Peggy's Cove?

    _____

16. In which province would you find totem poles?

    _____

 CANADA'S PROVINCES AND TERRITORIES

Lesson Plan #6: The Physical Regions of Canada

Expectations:

The students will:

- • identify the characteristics of the physical regions of Canada.
- • be able to locate regions on a map of Canada.
- • understand and use geographical terminology.

Discussion Time:

List the following geographical terms on the chalkboard, chart paper, or a white board. Discuss each term with your students. Beside each term, record its meaning. Complete the activity as a chart. Have the students make their own chart using the same headings and terms. The terms and meanings could be then copied onto their charts.

Geographical Terms

1. **bay**: a large, wide, deeply curved inlet along a coastline
2. **coastline**: the outline of a coast
3. **fiord**: a long, narrow bay of the sea bordered by steep cliffs
4. **glacier**: a large mass of ice formed from snow on high ground that moves down a mountain or along a sloping valley or spreading slowly over a large area of land until it melts or breaks up
5. **inlet**: a narrow strip of water running from a larger body of water into the land or between islands
6. **island**: a body of land completely surrounded by water
7. **lake**: a sizeable body of fresh or salt water surrounded by land
8. **lowland**: a low, flat region
9. **mountain**: a very high hill
10. **peak**: the pointed top of a mountain or hill
11. **peninsula**: a piece of land almost surrounded by water
12. **plain**: a flat stretch of land; prairie
3. **plateau**: a large high plain found near mountains
14. **river**: a large natural stream of water that flows into a lake, an ocean, or another river
15. **sea level**: the surface of the sea; landforms and ocean beds are measured as so many metres above or below sea level
16. **tundra**: a large region of treeless land between the permanent polar ice and the northern forests
17. **valley**: an area of low-lying land between mountains or hills; often has a river or stream flowing through it

CANADA'S PROVINCES AND TERRITORIES

Reproduce the Information Sheets entitled **"The Physical Regions of Canada"** pages 25 to 28 for the students to read independently or in a group. They could also be displayed on an overhead, on a white board, or used for your own general knowledge while teaching the topic. On the chalkboard or a chart, list the seven physical regions found in Canada. Explain to your students that the physical features of a country affect the way that people live and work.

Locate each region one at a time on a wall map. Have the students read the information for each region. Discuss the following items: location; land forms; minerals; vegetation; wildlife. After all the regions have been located and discussed, give your students the reproducible **Worksheet #1** on page 29 entitled **"Physical Regions of Canada."** Make the same chart on a chalkboard or a white board. The students will review each physical region and record the necessary information on the chart. Multiple charts will have to be reproduced for student usage.

Follow-Ups:
Reproduce the map entitled **"The Physical Regions of Canada"** found on page 30. The students will label the physical regions by recording each region's name in the empty box.

Answer Key for Worksheet #1: Physical Regions of Canada page 29. Answers will vary.

Answer Key for Map called Physical Regions of Canada page 30

1. Appalachian Region 2. The St. Lawrence Lowlands 3. The Hudson Bay Lowlands
4. The Canadian Shield 5. The Interior Plains 6. Rocky Mountains 7. Arctic Lowlands

 # Physical Regions of Canada

Canada has seven major land regions. They are:

- The Cordillera Region
- The Interior Plains or Lowlands
- The Hudson Bay Lowlands
- The Appalachian Region
- The Arctic Lowlands and the Innuitian Region
- The Canadian Shield
- The St. Lawrence Lowlands

The Cordillera Region

The Cordillera Region consists of the Pacific Coastal Mountain Ranges and Lowlands and the Rocky Mountains. Both of these regions consist of a very large group of mountains that extend from Alaska through to Mexico.

The Pacific Coastal Mountain Ranges and Lowlands

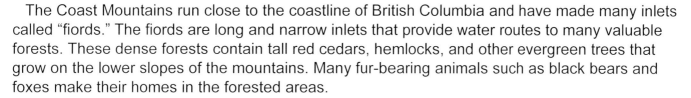

The Pacific Coastal Mountain Ranges and Lowlands are found in British Columbia and the southwestern part of the Yukon Territory. This region occupies almost all of British Columbia. The Queen Charlotte Islands and Vancouver Island are also included in this region. These islands are the top part of a mountain range that is partly covered by the Pacific Ocean. The Coast Mountains and St. Elias Mountains are found in this region also. Canada's highest Mountain, Mount Logan, is found in the St. Elias Mountains near the Alaskan border. It stands 5 951 metres above sea level. Glaciers cover many of the mountains found in the St. Elias Range.

The Coast Mountains run close to the coastline of British Columbia and have made many inlets called "fiords." The fiords are long and narrow inlets that provide water routes to many valuable forests. These dense forests contain tall red cedars, hemlocks, and other evergreen trees that grow on the lower slopes of the mountains. Many fur-bearing animals such as black bears and foxes make their homes in the forested areas.

East of the Coast Mountains lies an interior plateau that consists of valleys, plains, and small mountains. Many mineral resources such as "bismuth" and "molybdenum" have made this area very valuable. Farms, orchards, and grasslands for grazing cattle are found on the southern part of the interior plateau.

 ## The Rocky Mountains

The Rocky Mountains are located to the east of the Pacific Ranges and Lowlands. The mountains in the Rockies are often snow-capped and vary in height from 2 100 metres to 3 660 metres above sea level. Mount Robson is the tallest peak in eastern British Columbia and stands 3 954 metres high.

The Rocky Mountain Chain is 4 800 kilometres long and extends from New Mexico to Alaska. The Canadian Rockies stretch from Canada's southern border to the Laird River in British Columbia. The Selwyn Mountains and the Mackenzie Mountains are found between the Laird

River and the Alaskan border. In southern British Columbia, the Columbia Mountains are separated from the Canadian Rockies by a long, narrow valley called the Rocky Mountain Trench.

Rich deposits of coal, lead, silver, zinc, and other minerals are found in the Rocky Mountains. Large forests of juniper and pine trees grow on the Rockies' lower slopes. Firs and spruce are able to survive at higher elevations. Animals such as bears, deer, minks, mountain lions, squirrels, and many others live in the forests on the upper slopes. Above the timber line, an area where trees cannot grow, Rocky Mountain goats and bighorn sheep roam. Many types of fish inhabit the swift-flowing mountain streams.

The Arctic Lowlands and the Innuitian Region

The Arctic Lowlands are found within the Arctic Circle. The Arctic Lowlands consist of twelve large islands and hundreds of smaller ones. Most of the islands are barren and unexplored. Baffin Island and Ellesmere Island, which are two of the largest islands, have many glaciers, tall mountains, and fiords. Victoria Island is very flat. The seas around these many islands are frozen most of the year.

The Arctic Lowlands consist of tundras, which are areas too cold and dry for trees to grow. The subsoil is permanently frozen and only a thin layer thaws during the short, cool summers. Simple plants such as lichens, mosses, grasses and sedges grow in the lowlands. Caribou and musk oxen graze on the tundras. Other wildlife that make their homes in this region are Arctic foxes, Arctic hares, lemmings, polar bears, ptarmigans, seals, walruses, and whales. During the summer, insects thrive on the islands.

Petroleum and natural gas, lead, and zinc have been discovered in some of the western Arctic Islands but none of it has been taken out due to high production and transportation costs.

The Innuitian Region contains three mountain ranges. They are the Grantland, the Princess Margaret Range, and the Victoria and Albert Mountains. The terrain also contains plateaus, uplands, and lowlands. Many of these landforms are found on the Queen Elizabeth Islands. On some of the islands, the mountains are nearly buried by ice sheets. The only part that can be seen are their peaks which project like a row of nunataks.

The Interior Plains

The Interior Plains are located in the northern corner of British Columbia, most of Alberta and Saskatchewan, and the southwestern part of Manitoba. This regions extends north through the Northwest Territories to the Arctic Ocean.

The Interior Plains are covered in prairie grasslands in the south. The soil is rich and black and farmers grow wheat and other grains in it. In southern Alberta, the grasslands are used by ranchers for their cattle to graze on. The northern areas of the Interior Plains are heavily forested with white spruce and jack pine. Deer, elk, moose, and other fur-bearing animals

Physical Regions of Canada

inhabit the forested areas. Near the Arctic Ocean, the land becomes tundra covered by snow for more than half the year.

The Interior Plains are rich with many mineral deposits. Alberta has become a major mining area due to its large deposits of petroleum, natural gas, and coal. One of the world's largest tar sands (sands that contain oil) lies along the Athabaska River in Alberta. Important deposits of petroleum, uranium, and potash are found in southern Saskatchewan. In the Northwest Territories, petroleum, lead, and zinc have been found.

The Canadian Shield

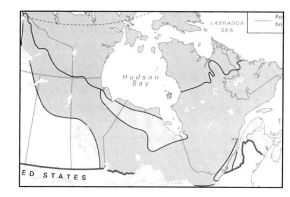

The Canadian Shield is a huge horseshoe-shaped region that curves around Hudson Bay from the Arctic Coast of the Northwest Territories to the coast of Labrador and the mainland of Newfoundland. It covers about one half of Canada and is made up of very old rock.

Thousands of lakes and rivers and many low hills are found in the Canadian Shield. The many rivers break into rapids and waterfalls at the edge of the region. Hydro-electric plants have been built on many rivers and supply hydro-electric power to many factories and homes in cities and towns in Québec, Ontario, and Manitoba.

Very few people live in the northern part of the Canadian Shield as the soil is poor and the climate is quite cold. Some northern areas of the Canadian Shield are tundra, and the plants and animals that live there are the same as the ones found in the Arctic Lowlands. The Canadian Shield is heavily forested in many northern areas. Deer, elk, moose, wolves, and smaller animals live in the forests.

The southern edge of the Canadian Shield does have soil that is good for farming. It is close to large cities such as Ottawa, Toronto, and Montreal. The many lakes and ski slopes in this area are used by the people who live in these cities. A great deal of Canada's mineral wealth is located in the Canadian Shield. Iron ore comes from mines in Québec. Cobalt, copper, gold, nickel, and uranium are mined near Sudbury, Ontario. The Canadian Shield also contains minerals such as platinum, silver, and zinc.

The Hudson Bay Lowlands

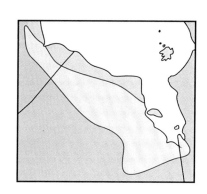

The Hudson Bay Lowlands are a flat, swampy region between the Canadian Shield and the southwestern coast of Hudson Bay. The Lowlands are covered with poor-quality forests and large deposits of peat, a decayed vegetable matter. There are very few settled areas in the lowlands. The only permanent settlements are small villages, trading posts, and ports such as Churchill and Moosonee.

Physical Regions of Canada

The St. Lawrence Lowlands

The St. Lawrence Lowlands is the smallest land region in Canada. More than half the people in Canada live in this region. The St. Lawrence Lowlands are made up of flat and rolling countryside along the St. Lawrence River and the Peninsula of Southern Ontario. It also includes the Island of Anticosti found at the mouth of the St. Lawrence River, which is a wilderness because it is isolated and has a colder climate.

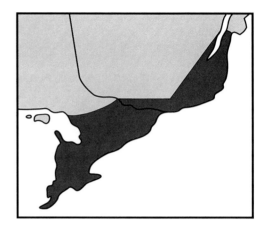

Canada's major deciduous forests are located in Southern Ontario. These trees shed their leaves every fall. The forests are filled with beech, hickory, maple, oak, and walnut trees. Many small animals such as squirrels, rabbits, raccoons, and porcupines inhabit the forested areas.

The St. Lawrence Lowlands is the major manufacturing centre of Canada because it has excellent transportation facilities and lies near markets in the eastern and central United States. Fertile soil and a mild climate allow farmers to grow many varieties of fruit and vegetables. Many dairy farms are located in this region.

The Appalachian Region

The Appalachian Region includes southeastern Québec and all of the Atlantic Provinces. The Appalachian Mountains are an ancient chain that extends from the island of Newfoundland and Labrador and south to the state of Alabama in the United States. The land in this region is generally hilly. Many of the mountains have been worn down by glaciers and erosion.The highest mountains are the Shickshock Mountains found in the Gaspé Peninsula in Québec.

Most of the people who live in the Appalachian Region make their homes along the Atlantic coast. Hundreds of bays and inlets provide excellent harbours for fishing boats. Parts of Newfoundland and Labrador and Nova Scotia have steep, rocky coastlines.

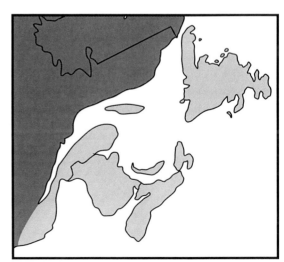

Evergreen trees and deciduous trees grow in the many forests found in the region. Good farmland is found in Prince Edward Island, along the St. John River in New Brunswick, and in the Annapolis River Valley in Nova Scotia. Québec has the world's richest deposits of asbestos. Coal and gypsum are mined in New Brunswick. Copper, lead, and zinc are mined in Newfoundland, Labrador, and New Brunswick.

Physical Regions of Canada

Worksheet # 1: Physical Regions of Canada

Physical Region: _____

Location	Land Forms	Minerals	Vegetation	Wildlife

Physical Region: _____

Location	Land Forms	Minerals	Vegetation	Wildlife

Physical Region: _____

Location	Land Forms	Minerals	Vegetation	Wildlife

SSJ192   ISBN 9781771586900

The Physical Regions of Canada

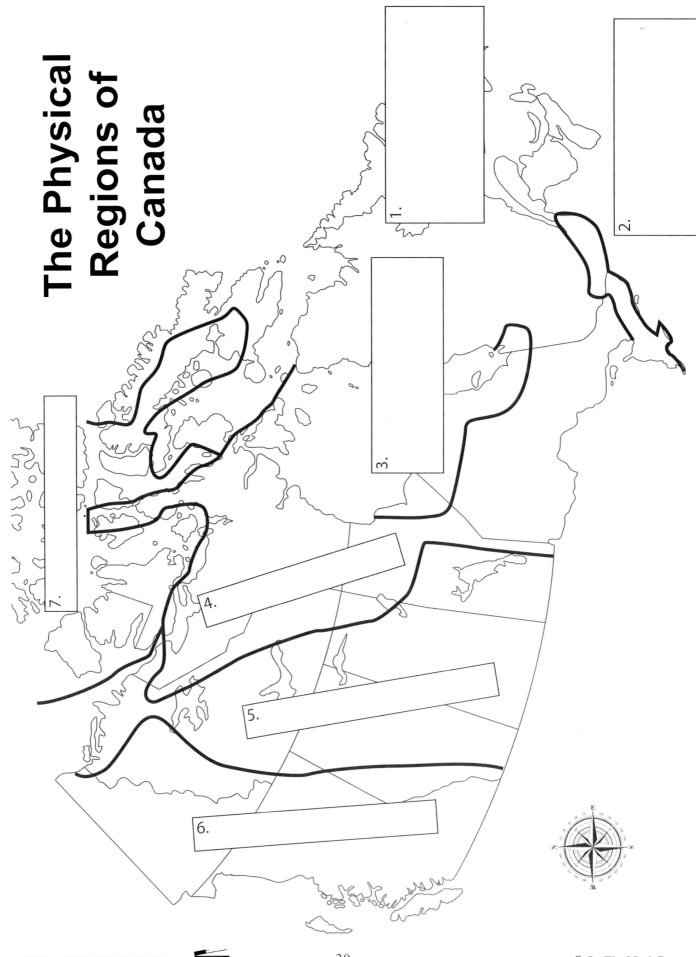

1.

2.

3.

4.

5.

6.

7.

Rivers of Canada

Lesson Plan #7: Rivers of Canada

Expectations:

The students will:

- identify and describe the main features of a river system.
- identify major rivers of Canada.
- demonstrate an understanding of the significance of the St. Lawrence River.
- understand the terms *mouth, source, branch, delta, flow, tributary, etc.*

Discussion Time:

Reproduce the Information Sheets entitled **"What is a River?"** pages 34 to 35 for your students to read, or display them on an overhead or white board. Read the information with the students and discuss the following terms. Record the terms on the chalkboard or a chart. Have the students give a meaning for each term. The students may copy the terms and their meanings on their own chart.

River Terms

1. **river:** a large body of flowing water that moves over the land in a long channel
2. **source of a river:** the beginning of a river, usually found in the mountains
3. **headwaters:** small streams found at the beginning of a river
4. **rills:** tiny, narrow channels of flowing water
5. **brooks:** wider and deeper channels of flowing water
6. **streams:** made from brooks joining together
7. **tributaries:** all the rills, brooks, and streams that carry water to a river
8. **river system:** of a river and all its tributaries
9. **drainage basin:** the area of land that a river system drains
10. **Continental Divide:** an imaginary line in the Rocky Mountains that divides North America into two large drainage basins
11. **river channel:** the land on either side of and beneath the flowing water
12. **river bed:** the bottom of the channel
13. **river banks:** the sides of the channel
14. **waterfalls:** a steep drop in the river's channel caused by erosion
15. **rapids:** water tumbling over large boulders in a river
16. **canyon:** a deep channel with high walls cut by a fast flowing river
17. **flood plain:** a flat area found on one or both sides of the banks of a river covered by water during a flood
18. **meander:** a snake-like bend in a river
19. **mouth of a river:** the place where the river empties its water into another body of water
20. **delta:** dirt and rock left by a river at its mouth to form a body of land
21. **river's load:** dirt and rock that the river carries as it travels to its mouth

---

Rivers of Canada

Follow-Ups:

1. Reproduce map entitled "**The Rivers of Canada**" on page 33 for each student or use it to make an overhead or on a white board for student viewing. The students are to locate the names of rivers on the map. Have them trace in blue each river that they find. Discuss the sizes and locations of as many rivers as you can.

2. Reproduce Worksheet #1 entitled "**Important Rivers of Canada**" page 37. The students are to complete the worksheet using the map entitled "The Rivers of Canada" found on page 33.

3. Reproduce Worksheet #2 entitled "**Where is Each River Located?**" on page 38. The student is to research to find the location of each river. They are to record the name of the province or territory on the line provided.

4. Reproduce Worksheet #3 entitled "**How Long Are the Rivers of Canada?**" page 39. The students are to arrange and record on the chart the names of the rivers in the order of size, from the largest to the smallest.

Answer Key for Worksheet #1: Important Rivers of Canada page 37

1. Ottawa River, St. Maurice River, Saguenay River 2. Albany River, Moose River, Rupert River, Eastmain River 3. Churchill River, Nelson River, Severn River, La Grande River 4. St. Lawrence River 5. Fraser River, Skeena River 6. North Saskatchewan River, South Saskatchewan River 7. Mackenzie River, Peel River, Coppermine River, Back River 8. Yukon River, Questions 9, 10, and 11 Answers will vary.

Answer Key for Worksheet #2: Where is Each River Located? page 38

1. Québec 2. Ontario 3. Ontario 4. Ontario 5. Alberta, British Columbia 6. British Columbia 7. Manitoba, Saskatchewan 8. Saskatchewan, Alberta 9. Ontario 10. Québec 11. Ontario, Québec 12. Ontario 13. Alberta, Northwest Territories 14. British Columbia 15. Ontario 16. British Columbia 17. Saskatchewan 18. British Columbia 19. New Brunswick 20. Newfoundland and Labrador

Answer Key for Worksheet #3: How Long are the Rivers in Canada? page 39

1. Mackenzie River – 4,241 km – Arctic Ocean 2. Yukon River – 3,185 km – Bering Sea 3. St. Lawrence River – 3,058 km – Atlantic Ocean 4. Columbia River – 2,000 km – Pacific Ocean 5. Peace River – 1,923 km – Lake Athabasca 6. Churchill River – 1,609 km – Hudson Bay 7. Fraser River – 1,370 km – Pacific Ocean 8. Ottawa River – 1,271 km – St. Lawrence River 9. Athabasca River – 1,231 km – Lake Athabasca 10. Laird River – 1,115 km – Mackenzie River.

The Rivers of Canada

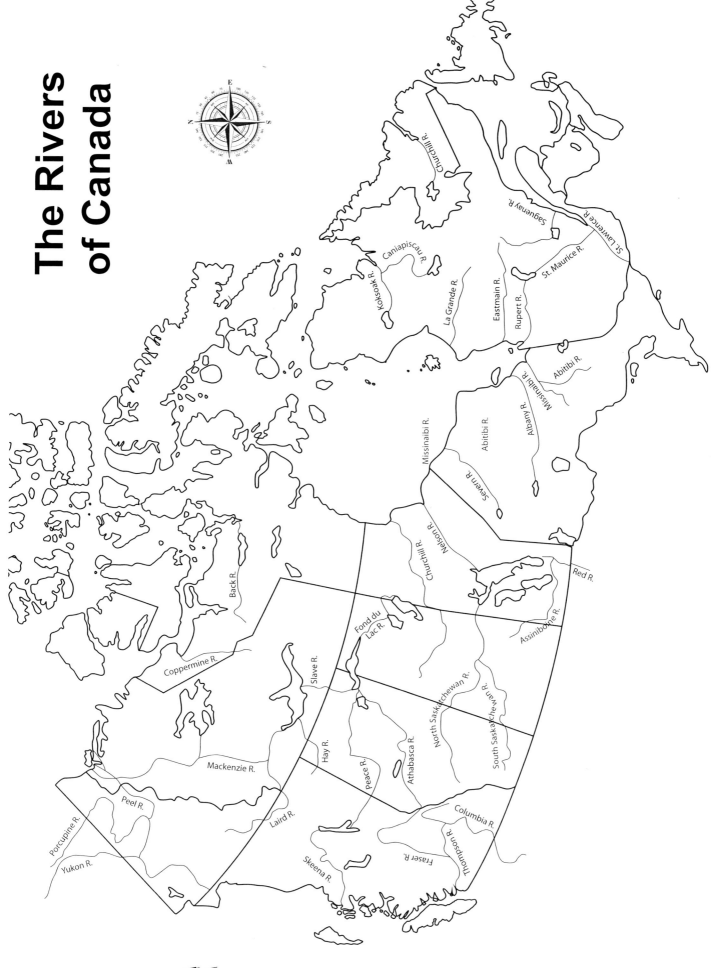

SSJ192   ISBN 9781771586900

What is a River?

A "river" is a large body of water that moves in a long channel. The "source" of a river usually begins high up in mountains or hills. The river's water comes from a combination of rainfall, lakes, springs, and melting ice and snow. Small streams flow from the river's source. These streams are called "headwaters." The headwaters flow into tiny narrow channels called "brooks." The brooks then join together to make "streams," and the streams join to form "rivers." All the rills, brooks, and streams that carry water to a river are called "tributaries." The river and its tributaries form a "river system." Some river systems have several small rivers that flow into larger ones.

Parts of a River System

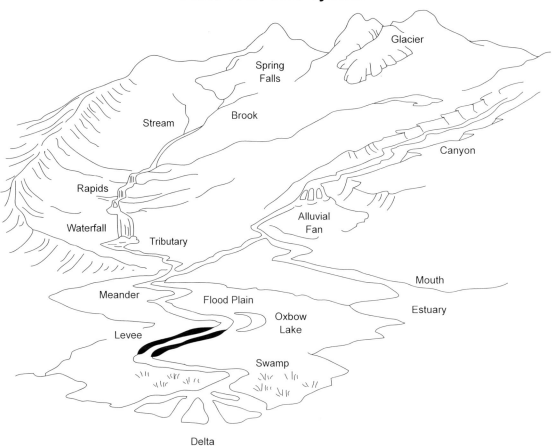

A river receives most of its water from rainfall. The rain flows over the land into the waters of the river system. The water eventually reaches the largest river in the system by way of rills, brooks, streams, and smaller rivers. The rain also soaks into the ground and gathers as ground water. The ground water seeps into the river system and keeps the water flowing in most rivers during dry periods.

The waters of a river system drain an area of land. This is called the system's "drainage basin." North America is split into two large drainage basins by an imaginary line called the "Continental Divide." Water from the eastern side of the divide flows toward the Atlantic Ocean, Arctic Ocean, or the Gulf of Mexico. Water from the western side of the divide flows toward the Pacific Ocean.

Rivers of Canada

The "channel" of a river consists of the land on either side of and beneath the flowing water. The bottom of the channel is the "bed" and the edges are the river "banks." The channel slopes steeply near the "source" of the river and almost flat at the "mouth." The flow of water of most rivers is faster in the middle course. The "mouth" of a river is where the river empties its waters into another body of water such as a lake, ocean, or larger river. The flow of the river's water slows down dramatically at the river's mouth. Sometimes this decrease in speed causes a body of land called a "delta" to form. Deltas are made of rock and dirt carried by the river. The rock and dirt settle where the river slows down. This material is called the river's "load."

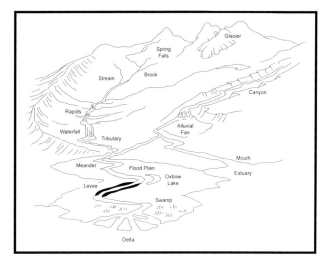

"Waterfalls" and "rapids" are found in a river. A waterfall occurs when the river crosses a layer of strong resistant rock. Downstream, the rock has been worn away by the river's flow which leaves a steep drop in the river's channel. The water passes over the edge of the harder layer and falls to the lower part of the channel.

"Rapids" occur when water tumbles over large boulders or rock ledges in the river channel. Fast-flowing rivers sometimes cut a canyon, which is a deep channel with high walls worn into the river's bed. A river's flow may also cut "valleys" through the land. The force of the river erodes the land to create a steep "v-shaped valley" that rises from the river's banks. A flat area may occur on one or both sides of the banks of a river. This area is called the "flood plain" and is covered by water during floods.

Some rivers have flood plains hundreds of kilometres wide. In a flood plain, the river channel tends to curve from one side of the plain to another. These snake-like bends are called "meanders."

There are many large rivers found in Canada. They are:

Athabasca River	Nelson River	Saint Mary's River	Churchill River
Niagara River	Saskatchewan River	Columbia River	Ottawa River
Skeena River	Detroit River	Peace River	Winnipeg River
Fraser River	Red River of the North	Yukon River	Mackenzie River
Restigouche River	Richelieu River	Miramichi River	Saguenay River
Saint John River	St. Lawrence River		

The Mackenzie River is the longest river in Canada and its length is 1,724 kilometres. The St. Lawrence River is the second longest measuring 1,300 kilometres.

The Rivers of Canada (no labels)

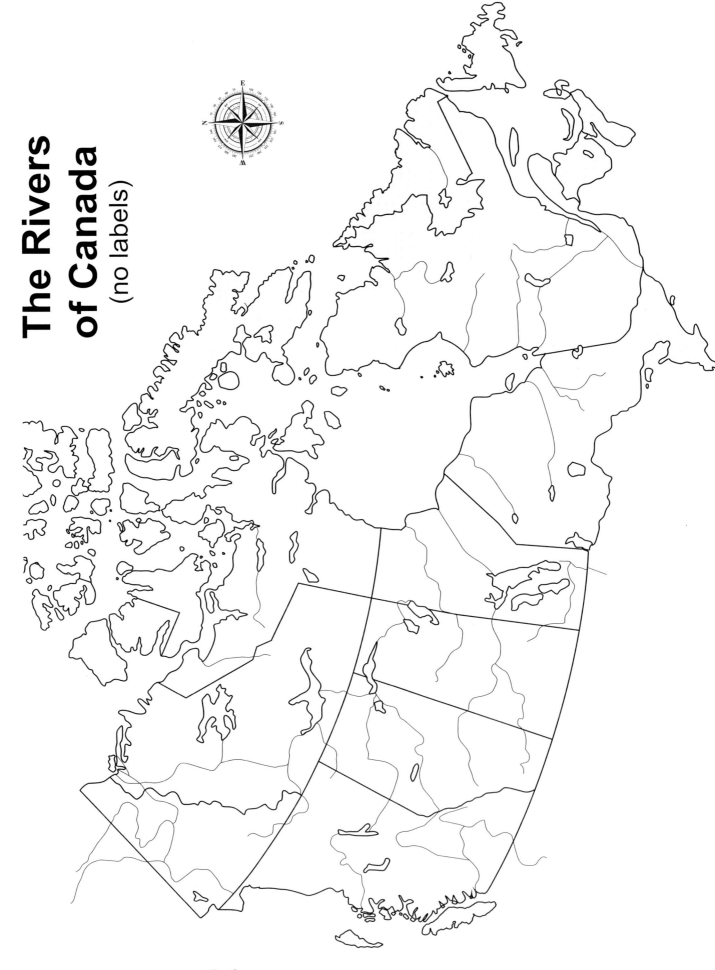

SSJ192 ISBN 9781771586900

Rivers of Canada

Worksheet #1: Important Rivers of Canada

1. Name three rivers that are tributaries of the St. Lawrence River.

_____

_____

2. Name four rivers that flow into James Bay.

_____

_____

3. Name four rivers that flow into Hudson Bay.

_____

_____

4. Which river has its source at Lake Ontario and its mouth at the Atlantic Ocean?

_____

_____

5. Name two rivers that flow into the Pacific Ocean.

_____

6. Which two rivers flow through the three prairie provinces?

_____

7. Name four rivers that flow north and empty into the Atlantic Ocean.

_____

_____

8. Name the river whose name is the same as a territory.

_____

9. On the map trace in blue all the rivers.
10. On the map circle in green the names of four rivers not entirely in Canada.
11. Underline in red the names of the rivers in your province or territory. Record their names on the lines below.

_____

_____

_____

_____

_____

SSJ192 ISBN 9781771586900

Rivers of Canada

Worksheet #2: Where Is Each River Located?

Using an atlas, locate the provinces and territories in which the following rivers are found.

1. Saguenay River _____

2. Trent River _____

3. Madawaska River _____

4. Abitibi River _____

5. Peace River _____

6. Fraser River _____

7. Nelson River _____

8. Saskatchewan River _____

9. Detroit River _____

10. Saint-Maurice River _____

11. Ottawa River _____

12. St. Clair River _____

13. Slave River _____

14. Skeena River _____

15. Thames River _____

16. Stikine River _____

17. Qu'Appele River _____

18. Thompson River _____

19. Saint John River _____

20. Gander River _____

Rivers of Canada

Worksheet #3: How Long Are The Rivers in Canada?

There are many freshwater rivers in Canada. Each river is a different length. On the chart below arrange the names of Canada's rivers from the largest to the smallest.

Canadian Rivers

Laird River	1,115 km	St. Lawrence River	3,058 km	Ottawa River	1,271 km
Fraser River	1,370 km	Columbia River	2,000 km	Peace River	1,923 km
Yukon River	1,231 km	Mackenzie River	4,241 km		
Churchill River	1,609 km	Athabasca River	1,231 km		

Name of River	Length in Kilometres	Flows Into
1.		
2.		
3.		
4.		
5.		
6.		
7.		
8.		
9.		
10.		

Lakes of Canada

Lesson Plan #8: Lakes of Canada

Expectations:

The students will:

- identify and locate major lakes of Canada.
- demonstrate an understanding of the significance of the Great Lakes.

Discussion Time:

Reproduce the Information Sheet #1 entitled **"What is a Lake?"** page 42 or use it to make an overhead or on a white board. The students will read the sheet and then locate the answers to the following questions.

1. Define a lake. (*a body of water surrounded by land*)
2. How were most lakes formed? (*glaciers carved deep valleys that filled up with water*)
3. From where do lakes get their water? (*fed by rivers, underground springs, or streams*)
4. Why are lakes important to communities? (*provide trade and travel; water used to irrigate farmers' fields; supply water to communities; generate electricity; used for recreation*)
5. Why are the Great Lakes famous? (*largest group of freshwater lakes in the world*)
6. What are the names of the lakes found in the Great Lakes System? (*Lake Ontario, Lake Erie, Lake Huron, Lake Superior, Lake Michigan*)
7. Locate the Great Lakes on the map. Have the students identify each one.
8. Which lakes are shared by Canada and the United States? (*Ontario, Erie, Huron, Superior*)
9. Which Great Lake is entirely in the United States? (*Lake Michigan*)
10. Into which river do the Great Lakes drain? (*St. Lawrence River*)
11. How was this inland waterway used years ago? (*It was the main route used by early explorers and settlers who lived in Canada and the United States.*)
12. Why did the areas around the St. Lawrence and the Great Lakes become highly industralized? (*Transportation was cheap.*)
13. What did Canada and the United States begin to build in 1954? (*The St. Lawrence Seaway*)
14. Why was the seaway built? (*It was built to allow ocean-going vessels to travel further inland by going around the rapids in the St. Lawrence River.*)
15. What else was built at the same time? (*hydro-electric power plants*)
16. Why did the people have to move from their homes and relocate somewhere else? (*The land was flooded and it became a reservoir called Lake St. Lawrence.*)
17. Which of the Great Lakes is the largest freshwater body in the world? (*Lake Superior*)
18. Which of the Great Lakes is the smallest? (*Lake Ontario*)
19. Which of the Great Lakes is the shallowest? (*Lake Erie*)

Follow-ups:

1. Reproduce the map entitled **"The Lakes of Canada"** found on page 43. Discuss how lakes are shown on a map. Have the students look for lakes in each province. They should also take note of the ones found in their own province or territory. Instruct the students to colour

Lakes of Canada

all the lakes that they can find in Canada blue. The lakes found in their own province or territory could be circled green. Have them star any lake that they have seen or travelled on in their own province or territory .

2. Reproduce the map entitled **"The Great Lakes"** found on page 44. Have the students locate each number on the map. In the box beside the number have the students neatly print the name of the lake, river, province, or country. Listed below are the places the students are to label on the map.
   1. *Lake Superior* ; 2. *Lake Michigan*; 3. *Lake Huron*; 4. *St. Clair River*; 5. *Lake St. Clair*; 6. *Detroit River*; 7. *Lake Erie*; 8. *Niagara River*; 9. *Lake Ontario*; 10. *St. Lawrence River*; 11. *Ottawa*; 12. *Province of Ontario*; 13. *St. Mary's River*; 14. *The United States of America*

3. Reproduce the Worksheet entitled **"Where Are the Lakes in Canada Found?"** located on page 45. Divide your class into groups of two or groups of four. Provide good Canadian atlases or maps for the students to use to locate the lakes listed on the worksheet. Some students could peruse the maps while others record the answers, or they all may search and record in a group.

Answer Key for Worksheet #1 "Where Are the Lakes in Canada Found?" page 45
a) Newfoundland: Grand Lake, Smallwood Reservoir
b) Québec: Lake St. John, Lake Abitibi, Lake Mistassini
c) Ontario: Lake Simcoe, Lake Ontario, Lake Nipissing, Lake Nipigon, Lake of the Woods, Lake St.Clair; Lake Huron; Lake Erie
d) Manitoba: Lake Winnipeg, Lake of the Woods, Lake Winnipegosis, Reindeer Lake
e) Saskatchewan: Lake Athabaska, Reindeer Lake
f) Alberta: Lake Louise, Lake Athabaska
g) British Columbia: Kootenay Lake, Lake Okanagan
h) New Brunswick: Grand Lake
i) Nunavut: Lake Garry, Lake Aberdeen
j) Northwest Territories: Great Slave Lake, Great Bear Lake

Lakes of Canada

What Is A Lake?

A lake is a body of water surrounded by land. The word "lake" comes from a Greek word which means "hole" or "pond." Most lakes were formed by glaciers. In the mountains, lakes were formed when glaciers carved deep valleys as they travelled. The basins they carved then filled up with water to form lakes. In other regions, glaciers gouged hollows in the land and deposited rocks and earth as they melted.

Lakes are fed by rivers and mountain streams. Some are fed by underground springs or streams. Some lakes have water running in, but none running out. Lakes provide trade and travel routes and water for farmers to use to irrigate their fields. They supply water to communities and are used to generate power. People also use them for recreational purposes.

The Great Lakes are the world's largest group of freshwater lakes. They are Lake Superior, Lake Michigan, Lake Huron, Lake Erie, and Lake Ontario. The Great Lakes form the most important inland waterway in North America. They were the main route used by early explorers and settlers who located in Canada and the United States. The areas along the Great Lakes and the St. Lawrence River became great industrial centres in Canada and the United States because transportation was cheap. Four of the Great Lakes are shared by Canada and the United States and they form a boundary between the two countries. Lake Michigan lies entirely in the United States. The Great Lakes drain into the St. Lawrence River.

Rapids on the St. Lawrence prevented large ocean vessels from travelling to ports on the Great Lakes. In 1954, Canada and the United States began to build the St. Lawrence Seaway. This project took five years to build. The Seaway was to become a major commercial waterway that would link the Atlantic Ocean and the Great Lakes. The Seaway was formed by the St. Lawrence River, several lakes, and a system of canals and locks. This waterway enables ocean-going vessels to travel further inland to ports located in Canada and the United States.

Power stations were also built to produce hydro-electric power to be used by both countries. Railways, highways, six villages and towns, and people had to be relocated as 16,000 hectares of land was going to be flooded in Ontario and New York State to create a new reservoir called Lake St. Lawrence. The reservoir would hold water to be used to make hydro-electric power. New communities were created near the reservoir.

In Canada you will find the following large freshwater lakes:

Lake Athabasca	Reindeer Lake	Lake Saint Clair	Lake Erie
Lake Superior	Lake Huron	Lake Nipigon	Lake Ontario
Lake Winnipeg	Lake Louise	Great Bear Lake	Lake Manitoba
Lake of the Woods	Lake Winnipegosis	Great Slave Lake	Smallwood Reservoir
Lesser Slave Lake			

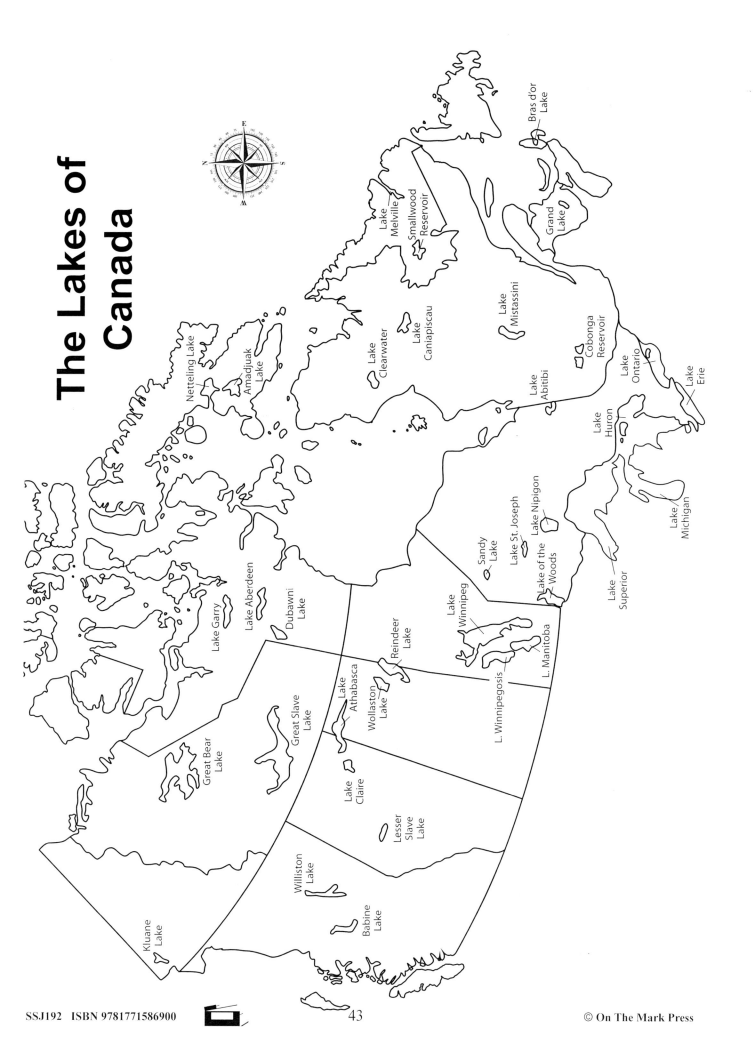

The Lakes of Canada

Bras d'or Lake

Lake Melville

Smallwood Reservoir

Grand Lake

Netteling Lake

Amadjuak Lake

Lake Clearwater

Lake Caniapiscau

Lake Mistassini

Cobonga Reservoir

Lake Abitibi

Lake Ontario

Lake Erie

Lake Huron

Lake Michigan

Lake Nipigon

Lake St. Joseph

Lake of the Woods

Lake Superior

Sandy Lake

Lake Winnipeg

Lake Garry

Lake Aberdeen

Dubawni Lake

Reindeer Lake

L. Manitoba

L. Winnipegosis

Great Bear Lake

Great Slave Lake

Lake Athabasca

Wollaston Lake

Lake Claire

Lesser Slave Lake

Williston Lake

Babine Lake

Kluane Lake

SSJ192 ISBN 9781771586900

The Great Lakes

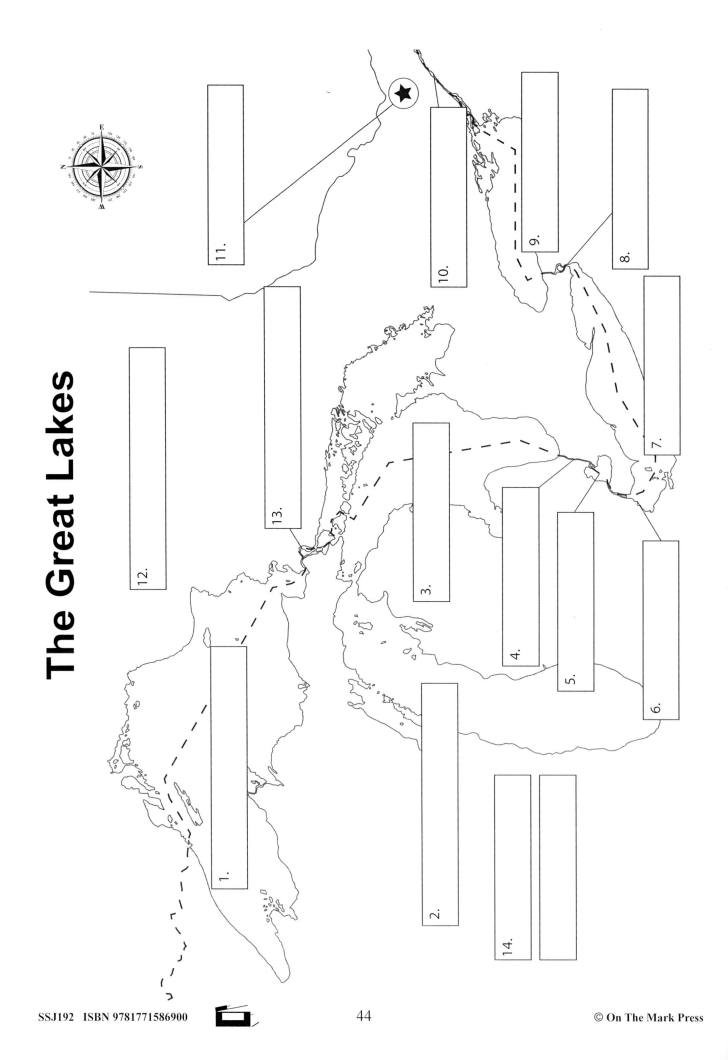

SSJ192 ISBN 9781771586900

Lakes of Canada

Worksheet #1: Where Are the Lakes In Canada Found?

Using an atlas, locate the provinces and territories in which the following lakes are found. Match each lake with the province (or provinces) it is located in.

Lake Louise	Lake Simcoe	Lake Huron	Lake Winnipeg
Lake Nipissing	Great Slave Lake	Lake Nipigon	Lake of the Woods
Lake Athabasca	Great Bear Lake	Lake St. John	Lake Abitibi
Lake St. Clair	Lake Winnipegosis	Grand Lake	Lake Mistassini
Lake Garry	Smallwood Reservoir	Lake Aberdeen	Reindeer Lake
Kootenay Lake	Lake Okanagan	Lake Ontario	Lake Erie

A. Newfoundland _____

_____

B. Québec_____

_____

C Ontario _____

_____

D. Manitoba_____

_____

E. Saskatchewan _____

_____

F. Alberta _____

_____

G. British Columbia _____

_____

H. New Brunswick_____

_____

I. Nunavut _____

J. Northwest Territories_____

_____

Canada's Population

Lesson Plan #9: Canada's Population

Expectations:

Students will:

- recognize the areas that are heavily populated in Canada and why.
- identify what affects population growth or decrease in growth.
- compare population in provinces and territories.
- interpret a population circle graph.
- read a map showing the distribution of the population of Canada.

A. Reproduce **Worksheets #1** called "**The Distribution of Canada's Population**" pages **48** to **49** for each student. Show the worksheet with the population distribution map on a white board. Discuss the map of Canada's Population and the areas in which people live. Work through the questions and have your students record responses to them on the lines provided.

Answer Key for Worksheet #1: The Distribution of Canada's Population pages 48 to 49:
1. They live in the southernmost areas of each province.
2. Ontario, Québec, British Columbia
3. It is warmer; better land; closer to the United States' markets; most cities are found here
4. Very few people live in the territories and the northern areas of the provinces.
5. Answers will vary.
6. They have good land for farming and grazing cattle.
7. This is the main water route to the west. Many cities are ports. There are many factories and places to work. The lakes provide good transportation.
8. They are very cold areas. You cannot farm or raise farm animals very well. They are isolated from the rest of the country. Some places do not have roads in or out connected to other places.
9. Answers will vary.
10. Answers will vary.

B. Reproduce **Worksheet #2** called "**Completing a Population Chart** located on **page 50** for each student to complete or show the same worksheet on a white board and complete sections **A** and **B** together as a large group.
Answer Key for **Part A** and **B** of **Worksheet #2** called "**Completing a Population Chart**" on **page 50**
Part A: Missing words: second; ten million; thirty-five million; uninhabited; rugged; severe
Part B: Nunavut – 31 906; Yukon Territory – 33 893; Northwest Territories – 41 462; Prince Edward Island – 140 204; Newfoundland and Labrador – 514 526; New Brunswick – 751 171; Nova Scotia – 931 727; Saskatchewan – 1 033 381; Manitoba – 1 208 268; Alberta – 3 645 257; British Columbia – 4 400 900; Québec – 7 903 001; Ontario – 12 851 821

C. Reproduce **Worksheet #3** called "**Reading a Chart**" found on page 51. Have students answer the questions using the completed population chart on page 50.

Canada's Population

Answer Key for Worksheet #3: Reading a Chart on page 51
1. Answers will vary. 2. Answers will vary. 3. Prince Edward Island 4. Ontario 5. Nunavut
6. 2 327 638 7. Northwest Territories 8. Nova Scotia 9. Saskatchewan 10. 5 886 906
11. 4 948 820 12. 374 332 13. No; Prince Edward Island

D. Reproduce the **Information Sheet #1** called **"Who Lives in Canada"** located on page 52 or display it on a white board for large group reading and discussion.
Discussion Questions:
1. What is Canada's population today? (*32 723 000*)
2. Why can Canada accommodate more people than the United States or Japan? (*It has more land area and not as many people for every square kilometre.*)
3. What has happened to Canada's population since World War Two? (*It has doubled in size.*) Give reasons why you think this has happened. (*Answers will vary.*)
4. Who lived in Canada at first? (*The First Nations People and the Inuit*)
5. From where did the rest of the people come? (*European countries*)
6. What is a refugee? (*Answers will vary.*) Why do refugees seek out Canada for a place to live? (*Answers will vary.*)
7. Name some of the countries and locate them on a map of the world. (*Britain, Germany, Greece, Italy, the Netherlands, Portugal, Latin America, China, Hungary, Ukraine, West Indies, Haiti, Trinidad*)
8. Think of the possible feelings early immigrants felt when they came to Canada. (*Answers will vary.*)
9. What are the two official languages spoken in Canada? (*French and English*)
10. Why do people from different nationalities speak their own native language in their homes? (*to preserve it*) Do you agree or disagree with this custom? (*Answers will vary.*)

E. Reproduce **Worksheet #4: Ethnic Population** located on **page 54**. Display the circle graph located on **Information Sheet #2** on **page 53** on a white board or duplicate the page for each student. Using the circle graph, have the students complete the worksheet.

F. **Answer Key** for **Worksheet #4** called **Ethnic Population** on **page 54**
1. White 2. No, same amount 3. White, French, German 4. Portuguese, Latin American, Scandinavian, Russian, Jewish 5. No, same amount

Ethnic Populations from Largest to Smallest:
White, French, German, East Asian, Chinese, Italian, Aboriginal, Ukrainian, Dutch, Polish, Black, Scandinavian, Russian, Latin American, Jewish, Portuguese

Canada's Population

Worksheet #1: Distribution of Canada's Population

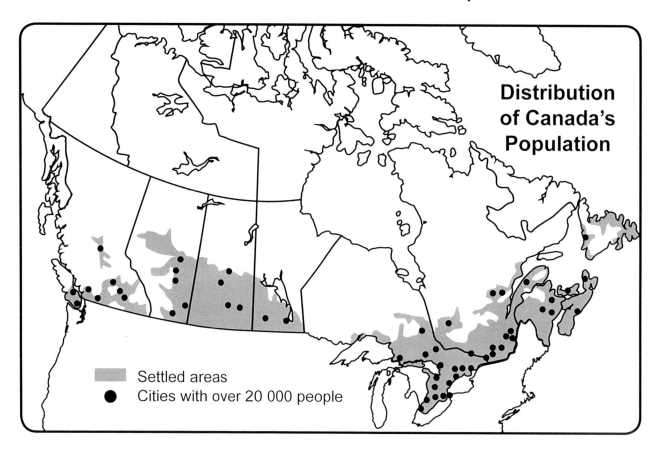

Distribution of Canada's Population

Settled areas
● Cities with over 20 000 people

1. Where do most of the people in Canada live?

_____

_____

2. In which three provinces do you find the most cities with over 20 000 people?

_____

_____

3. Why do you think most of the people live in these areas?

_____

_____

4. In which areas do very few people live?

_____

_____

Canada's Population

Worksheet #1: The Distribution of Canada's Population

5. There are some areas across central and northern Canada that are settled. Why do you think people live there? Give four good reasons.

_____

_____

_____

_____

6. Why is the southern half of Alberta, Saskatchewan, and Manitoba a popular place to live?

_____

_____

_____

_____

7. Why do the areas close to the Great Lakes have so many large cities?

_____

_____

_____

_____

8. Why are the three territories so sparsely populated?

_____

_____

_____

_____

9. Describe the density of the population in the area in which you live. List the ethnic backgrounds that make up the area.

_____

_____

_____

_____

_____

10. Eventually some areas will become over-populated. What do you think the government should do to prevent over-population?

_____

_____

_____

_____

SSJ192 ISBN 9781771586900

Canada's Population

Worksheet #2: Completing A Population Chart

A. Canada is the _____ largest country in the world with nearly _____ square kilometres of land. Its population is over _____. About seventy-five percent of the people live within one hundred and fifty kilometres of the southern border. Much of Canada is _____ because the country's terrain is _____ and its climate is quite _____ in northern areas.

B. Listed below are the names of the provinces and territories in Canada and their populations. Complete the empty chart by listing the provinces and territories according to population from the smallest to the largest.

Province/Territory	Population	Province/Territory	Population
Newfoundland & Labrador	514 536		
Prince Edward Island	140 204		
New Brunswick	751 171		
Nova Scotia	921 727		
Québec	7 903 001		
Ontario	12 851 821		
Manitoba	1 208 268		
Saskatchewan	1 033 381		
Alberta	3 645 257		
British Columbia	4 400 900		
Yukon Territory	33 897		
Northwest Territories	41 462		
Nunavut	31 906		

Canada's Population

Worksheet #3: Reading A Chart

Using the facts on the chart that you have just organized, answer the following questions about Canada's population.

1. Star the province or territory in which you live and circle its population on the chart that you completed. What is the name of your province/territory and what is its population?

   _____

   Where does your province or territory rank with the other provinces and territories?

   _____

2. How does your province or territory rate in the size of its population?

   _____

3. Which province has the smallest population in Canada?

   _____

4. Which province is the most populated?

   _____

5. Which of the territories has the lowest population?

   _____

6. What is the total population of the Atlantic Provinces?

   _____

7. Which of the territories has the largest population?

   _____

8. Which of the Atlantic Provinces has the highest population?

   _____

9. Which of the Prairie Provinces has the highest population?

   _____

10. What is the total population of the Prairie provinces?

    _____

11. What is the difference between Ontario's and Québec's population?

    _____

12. How many more people live in Newfoundland/Labrador than in Prince Edward island?

    _____

13. Does the total population of the three territories equal the population of Prince Edward Island? _____ Which area has the larger population?

    _____

Canada's Population

Information Sheet #1

Who Lives in Canada?

There are approximately 32,723,000 people living in Canada today. Canada is the second largest country in the world and has an area of ten million square kilometres. There is an average of three people for every square kilometre. Compare that to the United States where there are twenty-eight people per square kilometre, and Japan where there are 335 people per square kilometre

Since World War Two, Canada's population has doubled. Almost all Canadians are of European descent. The First Nations People and the Inuit make up about two percent of the nation's population. The Inuit live mainly in Nunavut and the northern areas of the Northwest Territories, Newfoundland and Labrador, and Ontario.

The First Nations People belong to one of ten major groups such as the Algonkian, the Athapaskan, the Haida, the Iroquoian, the Kootenayan, the Salishan, the Siouan, the Tlingit, the Tsimshian and the Wakashan. The majority of the First Nations People live on reserves or reservations across Canada.

Early immigrants came from Britain, Germany, Greece, Italy, the Netherlands, Portugal, and Latin America. Many Canadians are refugees from other countries who were involved in revolutions. These people came from Hungary, Cambodia, Laos, and Vietnam. Since Hong Kong was given back to China by the British, many Chinese immigrants came to Canada and lived in the Toronto area and in British Columbia. The Prairie Provinces were settled mainly by Ukrainians and Germans. Many black immigrants of West Indian descent who came from French and English islands such as Haiti and Trinidad have made their homes in Canada as well.

In Canada, two official languages are spoken. They are French and English. French is mainly spoken in Québec while English is mainly used in the rest of the country. Other languages are often spoken in the homes of different nationalities in order to maintain and preserve the language.

Canada's Population

Ethnic Population of Canada

Canada's population is made up of many cultures and people. These immigrants and their descendents came from various countries around the world.

Look at the population circle graph to find out who lives in Canada.

Total Population By Ethnic Origin

Examine the population map of Canada carefully.

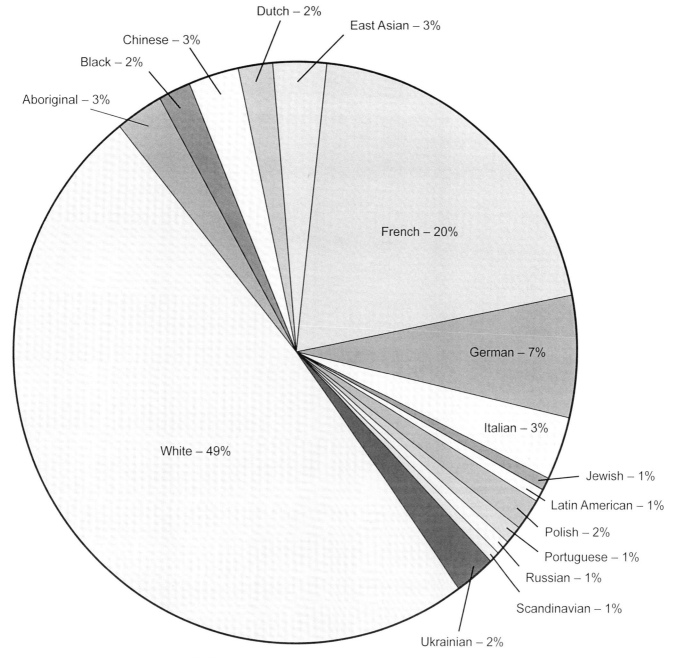

Dutch – 2%

East Asian – 3%

Chinese – 3%

Black – 2%

Aboriginal – 3%

French – 20%

German – 7%

Italian – 3%

White – 49%

Jewish – 1%

Latin American – 1%

Polish – 2%

Portuguese – 1%

Russian – 1%

Scandinavian – 1%

Ukrainian – 2%

Canada's Population

Worksheet #4: Ethnic Population

Use the circle graph to locate the answers to the following questions.

1. Of what descent are most of the people in Canada? _____
2. Are there more Aboriginal people than Chinese living in Canada? _____
3. What are the three largest ethnic groups found in Canada? _____
_____
4. What are the three smallest ethnic groups found in Canada? _____
5. Are there more Dutch people than Ukrainian people in Canada? _____

Ethnic Populations

Rank the ethnic populations from 1 to 16. Record the population and each group from the largest to the smallest.

Aboriginal 1 400 685 _____

Black 945 665 _____

Chinese 1 487 580 _____

Dutch 1 035 965 _____

East Asian 1 553 150 _____

French 10 421 365 _____

German 3 445 335 _____

Italian 1 445 335 _____

Jewish 358 000 _____

Latin American 381 280 _____

Polish 984 585 _____

Portuguese 282 865 _____

Russian 500 600 _____

Scandinavian 714 000 _____

Ukrainian 1 209 085 _____

White 25 186 893 _____

The ethnic group with the largest population is _____.

The ethnic group with the smallest population is _____.

Canada's Climate

Lesson Plan #10: Climatic Regions of Canada

Expectations:

Students will:
- recognize the climatic changes in Canada from east to west and north to south.
- understand how physical features affect climate.
- identify climatic regions in Canada.
- compare temperatures in different locations in Canada.
- interpret a bar graph for information.
- identify the climate in their own community.

A. Reproduce the **Information Sheet** called **"Climatic Regions of Canada"** found on **page 56** for your students to read or display it on a white board for large group reading. Discuss the six climatic regions in Canada and list their names on a chart. Circle the climatic region in which the students live.

B. Reproduce **Worksheet #1** called **"Climatic Regions of Canada"** found on **page 57** for your students to complete independently. They will need to refer to **Information Sheet #1** called **Climatic Regions of Canada** found on **page 56** for the answers to "Which region is it?"

   Answer Key for "Which region is it? page 57
   1. Pacific Region 2. Arctic Region 3. Northern Region 4. Prairie Region 5. Mountain Region
   6. Southeastern Region

C. Reproduce the map called **"Climatic Map of Canada"** found on **page 58** for your students or display it on a White Board for the students to use while completing the exercise called **"Let's Compare Temperatures!"** on **page 57**.

   Discuss the different temperatures in the various areas and what may affect them.

   Have the students complete the section of **Worksheet #1** called **"Let's Compare Temperatures!"**

   Answer Key for "Let's Compare Temperatures!" page 57
   1. No 2. - 8° 3. 16° 4. - 23° 5. Resolute 6. Prince Rupert is closer to the ocean. Kamloops is further south and Prince George is in the mountains. 7. Yellowknife 8. Victoria, Moosonee

D. Reproduce **Worksheet #3** called **"Precipitation and Temperature"** on **page 60** for the students to use with the bar graph on **page 59** or display the bar graph on a white board. The students will record their answers to the questions on **page 60**.

   Answer Key for Questions about Precipitation and Temperature page 60
   1. Winnipeg 2. Yellowknife 3. Victoria 4. St. John's 5. Winnipeg 6. St John's, Halifax
   7. St. John's, Halifax, Charlottetown, Fredericton, Québec City, Toronto 8. Whitehorse, Yellowknife

   Answer Key for Community Climate page 60: Answers will vary.

Canada's Climate

Information Sheet #1

Climatic Regions of Canada

Canada's climate changes as you travel from east to west and even from south to north.

In the Mountain Region on the western coast of Canada, the winter and summer conditions vary greatly in different parts of the region. Valleys and southern areas are generally warmer than in the mountains and northern areas. Precipitation is also varied. The western slopes of the mountains usually receive more precipitation than the eastern slopes.

In the Pacific Region, the winters are mild with temperatures above freezing. Summers are warm. Precipitation is quite heavy and comes mainly in the winter.

The Prairie Region has very cold winters and hot, dry summers. Precipitation is light and comes mainly in the summer.

The Arctic Region has extremely cold winters which last eight to ten months. Precipitation is very light.

The Northern Region of Canada has cold winters that last up to six months. Summers are cool and short. Precipitation is moderate and occurs mainly in the summer.

The Southeastern Region has cold winters in the central area and milder ones in the southwest area. Summers are usually warm. A moderate amount of rainfall is experienced.

SSJ192   ISBN 9781771586900   56   © On The Mark Press

Canada's Climate

Worksheet #1: Climatic Regions of Canada

Which region is it?

> Southeastern Region   Prairie Region   Pacific Region
> Northern Region   Arctic Region   Mountain Region

1. Its winters are mild and its temperatures seldom go below freezing.

   _____

2. Its winters last eight to ten months and are extremely cold.

   _____

3. The winters are cold and last up to six months. Summers are short and cold.

   _____

4. This region has very cold winters with hot, dry summers.

   _____

5. Valleys are warmer than the mountains and northern areas.

   _____

6. Winters are cold in one area and mild in another.

   _____

Let's Compare Temperatures!

Look at the "Climatic Map of Canada." Locate the different temperatures of the cities that are labelled. Answer the following questions.

1. Is Prince Rupert, British Columbia colder than Moosonee, Ontario in the winter? _____
2. How much colder is Ottawa in the winter than Niagara Falls? _____
3. What is the temperature of Victoria, British Columbia in the summer? _____
4. What is the difference in temperature between Iqaluit and Halifax in the summer? _____
5. Which place in Canada has the coldest summer and winter? _____
6. Why do you think Prince George is colder in the winter than Prince Rupert and Kamloops?

   _____
   _____

7. Which city is -29° C in the winter and 15° C in the summer?

   _____

8. Which two places have the same temperature in the summer?

   _____

Climate Map of Canada

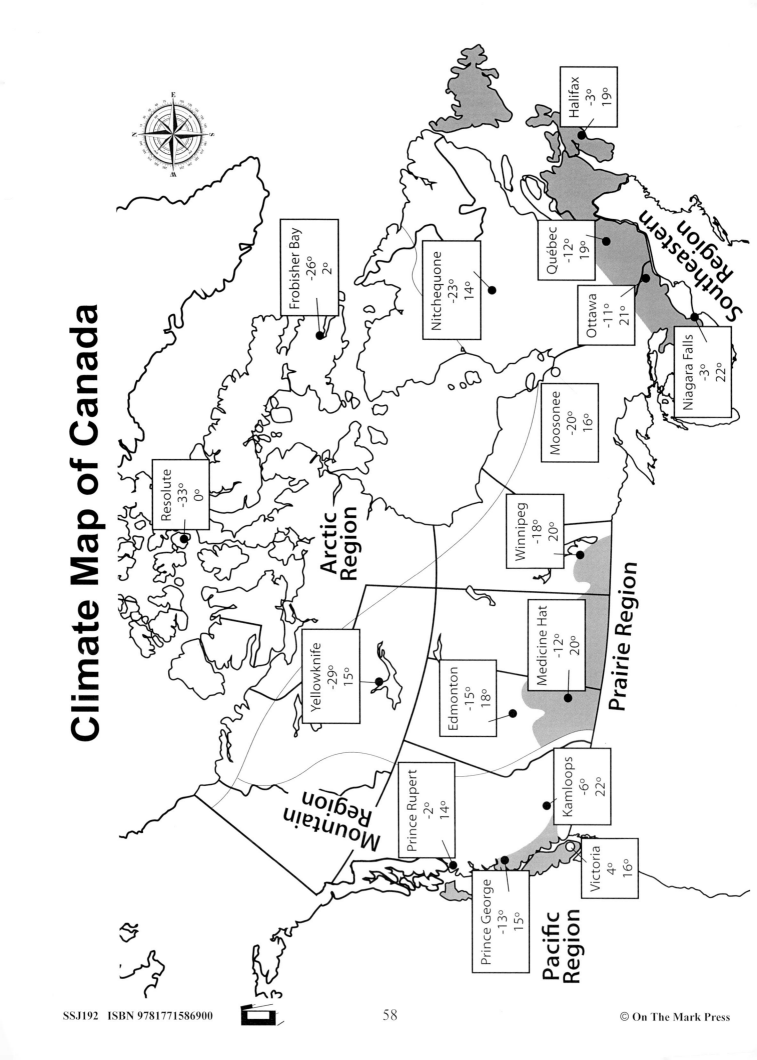

Resolute
-33°
0°

Frobisher Bay
-26°
2°

Nitchequone
-23°
14°

Québec
-12°
19°

Halifax
-3°
19°

Ottawa
-11°
21°

Niagara Falls
-3°
22°

Moosonee
-20°
16°

Winnipeg
-18°
20°

Yellowknife
-29°
15°

Edmonton
-15°
18°

Medicine Hat
-12°
20°

Prince Rupert
-2°
14°

Kamloops
-6°
22°

Victoria
4°
16°

Prince George
-13°
15°

Arctic Region

Prairie Region

Southeastern Region

Mountain Region

Pacific Region

SSJ192 ISBN 9781771586900

Canada's Climate

Precipation and Temperature

The bar graph below shows the precipitation and temperature ranges for most of the capital cities of Canada.

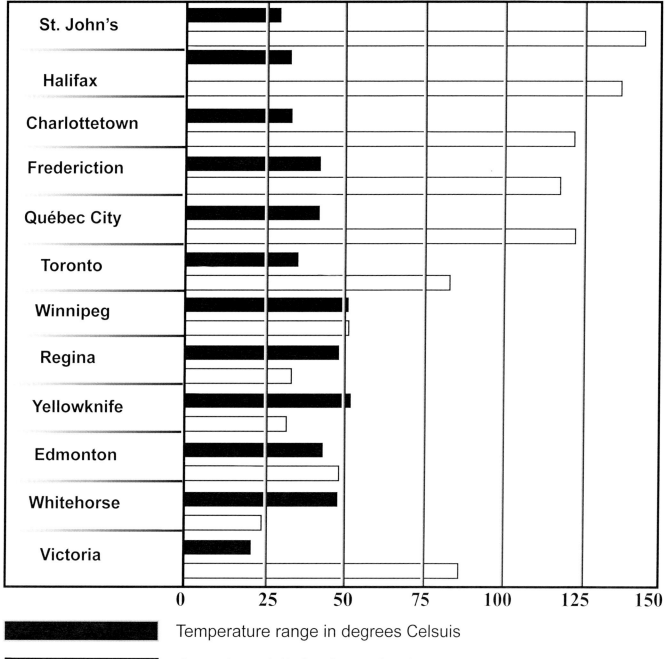

Temperature range in degrees Celsuis

Annual precipitation in centimetres

SSJ192 ISBN 9781771586900 59

Canada's Climate

Worksheet #3: Precipitation and Temperature

Examine the graph carefully and then answers the following questions.

1. Which capital city received 50 centimetres of rain? _____

2. Which capital city has the highest temperature range? _____

3. Which capital city had the lowest range in temperature? _____

4. Which capital city received the most rainfall? _____

5. Which city has the same range in temperature and annual rainfall? _____

6. Which two cities receive more than 125 centimetres of rainfall each year?

_____

7.How many cities receive more than 75 centimetres of rainfall each year?

_____

_____

8. Which cities receive less than 25 centimetres of rain each year?

_____

Community Climate

Find out the following things about your local community:

1. What is the average temperature in your community during the summer? _____

2. What is the average temperature in your community in the winter? _____

3. What is the average temperature in your community in the spring? _____

4. What is the average temperature in your community in the autumn? _____

5. How many centimetres of rainfall does your community receive in a year? _____

6. How many centimetres of snowfall does your community receive in a year? _____

7. What is the highest temperature that your community has ever experienced during a

    summer? _____

8. What is the coldest temperature that your community has ever experienced during a winter?

_____

Canada's Natural Vegetation

Lesson Plan # 11: Canada's Natural Vegetation

Expectations:

Students will:
- recognize the vegetation regions located in Canada.
- understand that location and climate affect the types of vegetation that can grow in certain areas.
- identify the vegetation zone in which they live.

A. Reproduce the **Information Sheets #1** called **"Canada's Natural Vegetation"** found on **pages 63 to 64** for your students to read independently or display them on a white board for large group reading and discussion.

The following questions could be asked during the discussion.
1. How many different vegetation zones are there in Canada? *(14)* What are the three major zones? (*forest, grassland, tundra*)

2. Describe the Arctic Tundra Region. (*very few plants grow; four major plant communities are lichens, Arctic poppies, saxifrage, mountain avens; very few trees*) Why does so little plant-life exist in the Arctic Tundra? (*lack of moisture, poor soil, cold climate*)

3. Which zone is called "the land of little sticks?" (*Subarctic or Transition Forest Region*) What is happening to the vegetation in this area? (*It is changing to open forests where trees are small and stunted.*)

4. What grows in the Taiga or Boreal Forest Region? (*mainly coniferous trees such as spruce, balsam, fir, pine*) Why do you think larger trees grow in this area? (*The climate is warmer and wetter.*)

5. How are the forests in the Pacific Coast Forest Region and the Columbia Forest Region similar? (*The same types of trees grow in both areas.*)

6. Which vegetation zone is made up of grassland and pine trees? (*The Mountain Forest Region*)

7. Which vegetation zone has trees used for pulp and paper? (*Rocky Mountain Forest Region*)

8. Which forest zone is above the tree-line? (*The Alpine Forest Region*)

9. In which area are white spruce, aspen, and balm of Gilead found? (*The Mixed Woods Region*)

10. Why is the Parkland called a transition area? (*The forest changes into a grassland.*)

11. What mainly grows in the Prairie Region? (*various kinds of grasses*) Why do the grasses in this area have deep root systems? (*The roots search for water in the soil.*) Do you think this area receives a lot of moisture? (*No*) Why? (*because of the plants, deep root systems that are looking for water*)

Canada's Natural Vegetation

12. Which zone has deciduous trees and coniferous trees? (*The Great Lakes – St. Lawrence Lowlands*) Why are both types of trees able to grow in this zone? (*It has the right climate.*) Why are these forests so valuable? (*for their timber*)

13. Which zone is similar in vegetation to The Niagara Region? (*The Acadian Forest*)

14. In which vegetation zone do we live? (*Answers will vary.*)

B. Reproduce the map called **"Natural Vegetation Regions of Canada"** found on **page 65** for your students or display it on a White Board for all to see.

Reproduce **Worksheet #1** called **"Natural Vegetation Regions of Canada"** found on page 66 for your students to complete independently using the information they locate from the map.

C. Answer Key for Worksheet #2: Natural Vegetation Regions of Canada found on page 66

1. coniferous, deciduous
2. low shrubs, mosses, lichens
3. British Columbia
4. Alberta, Saskatchewan, Manitoba
5. Northwest Territories, Nunavut, Ontario, Québec, Newfoundland and Labrador,
6. Newfoundland and Labrador, Nova Scotia, New Brunswick, Québec, Ontario, Saskatchewan
7. Yukon, British Columbia, Alberta
8. A coniferous tree bears needles and its seeds are found in its cones. It does not lose its needles every year. Coniferous trees are spruce, pine, and hemlock.
9. A decidous tree bears leaves and then loses them in the autumn of every year. Deciduous trees are maple, elm, and beech.
10. It is a large treeless area found above the treeline.

Canada's Natural Vegetation

Information Sheet #1

What Grows in Canada?

Forest, grassland, and tundra are the major vegetation zones in Canada. There are fourteen different vegetation zones. They are:

Arctic Tundra	Subarctic or Transition Forest	Rocky Mountain Forest
Mixed Woods	Great Lakes – St. Lawrence Forest	Acadian Forest
Niagara Forest	Taiga or Boreal Forest	Columbia Forest
Mountain Forest	Pacific Coast Forest	Alpine Forest
The Prairies	Parkland	

The *Arctic Tundra Region* has very few trees due to a lack of moisture, poor soil, and a cold climate. Four major plant communities are found in the Arctic Tundra Region. They are rock desert, tundra-heath, strand, and freshwater. A variety of Arctic flowers such as Arctic poppies, saxifrage, and mountain avens can be seen during the summer. They create a colourful landscape.

The *Subartic or Transition Forest Region* is the transition stage where open forest and stunted growth create the "land of the little sticks."

The *Taiga or Boreal Forest Region* consists of white and black spruce, balsam, fir, and jack pine which grow in the eastern and central areas. Alpine fir and lodgepole pine are found in the west and northwest.

The *Pacific Coast Forest Region* has large coniferous trees due to the mild, humid climate. The main species are western red cedar, western hemlock, sitka spruce, and Douglas fir.

The *Columbia Forest Region* is found in the Selkirk and Monashee Mountains. This area is quite wet and the trees are similar to the ones that grow in the Pacific Coast Forest.

The *Mountain Forest Region* is composed of grassland and scattered stands of Ponderosa Pine. This type of forest grows in the valleys of the central plateau of British Columbia where drought conditions are often experienced.

The *Rocky Mountain Forest Region* is found on the foothills and the lower mountain slopes. The main species are Engelmann spruce, alpine fir, lodgepole pine, and aspen. These forests are mainly used for pulp and paper.

The *Alpine Forest Region* includes all the mountain areas above the tree line. Meadow and tundra-like plants are quite common in this area.

The *Mixed Woods Region* is found near the Taiga or Boreal Region. White spruce, aspen, and balm of Gilead are the species found in this region.

The *Parkland* is a transition area between the forest proper and the prairie grassland. Aspen are seen growing here.

The *Prairie Region* is divided into a short-grass zone and a mixed grass zone. The types of grasses that grow depend upon the amount of available moisture in the ground. Prairie grasses

Canada's Natural Vegetation

Information Sheet #2

form a tough sod because they have a dense root system that searches for water in the soil. Grasses such as blue gamma grass, common spear grass, western wheat grass, prairie blue grass, and June grass are common. Sage brush and prickly pear cactus also grow in the region.

The *Great Lakes - St. Lawrence Forest* contains a wealth of species. This region's climatic conditions and accessibility make these forests one of the most valuable timber resources. This region supports conifers as well as deciduous trees. Conifers are white pine, red pine, and white spruce. Deciduous trees found in this region are sugar maple, beech, red oak, and red maple.

The *Niagara Region* is the eastern deciduous forest region. Species that grow in the Great Lakes-St. Lawrence Forest Region grow here as well as black walnut, scarlet oak, sassafras, magnolia, tulip tree, sycamore, and Kentucky coffee tree which usually grows in more southern climates.

The *Acadian Forest* of Nova Scotia, Prince Edward Island, and southern New Brunswick is similar to the Great Lakes Forest region. White spruce, white pine, red pine, and red spruce are types of conifers found as well as deciduous hardwoods such as maple, birch, and beech.

Taiga

Deciduous

Grasslands

Tundra

SSJ192 ISBN 9781771586900   64

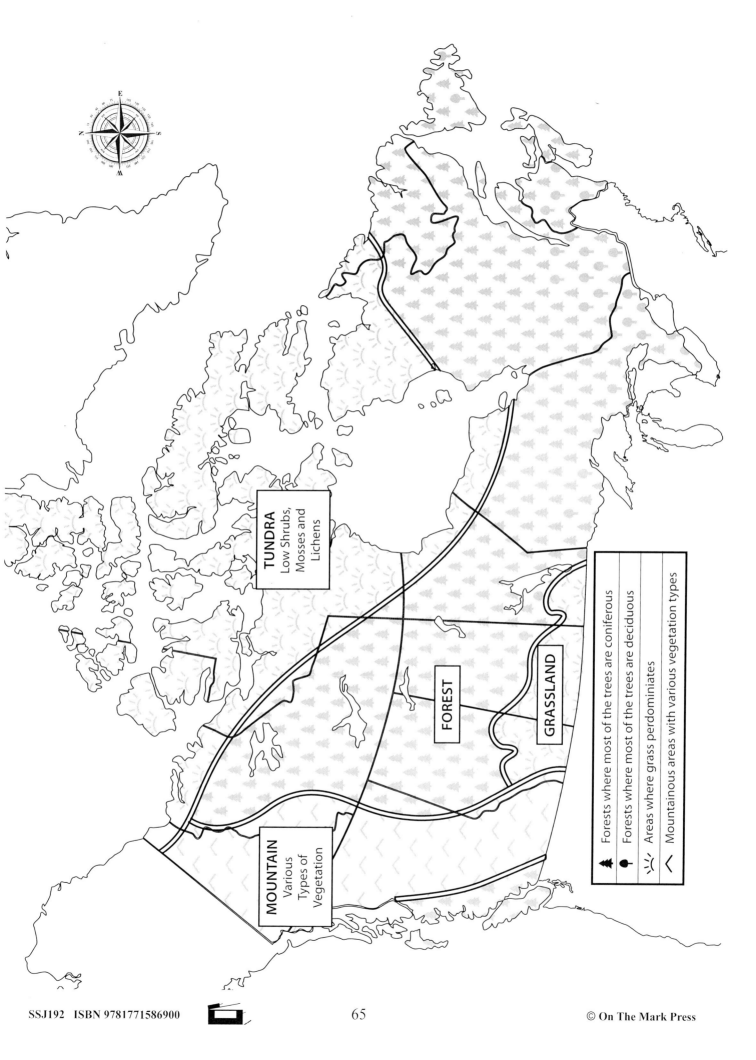

SSJ192   ISBN 9781771586900

Canada's Natural Vegetation

Worksheet #1: Natural Vegetation Regions of Canada

Throughout Canada, different types of vegetation are able to grow despite of its diversified climate.

Examine the map entitled "**Natural Vegetation Regions of Canada**."

Locate the answers to the following questions.

1. What types of trees grow in Newfoundland and Labrador? _____
_____

2. What types of vegetation grow above the treeline? _____
_____

3. In which province are the trees tall and the forests dense? _____

4. Which provinces have grasslands? _____
_____

5. In which territories and provinces would you find tundra? _____
_____
_____

6. In which provinces would you find deciduous trees growing? _____
_____
_____

7. Which provinces and which territory have a variety of things growing in the mountains?
_____
_____

8. What is a coniferous tree? _____
_____

   Name three coniferous trees that grow in Canada. _____
_____

9. What is a deciduous tree? _____
_____

   Name three deciduous trees that grow in Canada. _____
_____

10. What is tundra? _____
_____

The Atlantic Provinces

Lesson Plan #12: The Atlantic Provinces

Expectations:

Students will:
• become more knowledgeable and better acquainted with the area's location; provinces; physical features; climate; bodies of water; agriculture; mineral resources; fishing; cities in the Atlantic Provinces; symbols and flags of each province.
• develop reading and research skills to locate answers requested by various questions.
• identify and label a map of the Atlantic Provinces.

A. Reproduce **Information Sheet #1** called **"The Atlantic Region"** found on **page 69** for your students to read independently or display it on a white board for large group reading and discussion.

Brainstorm for facts the students may already know about the "Atlantic Region."

Have your students read the information in each paragraph. Then have a student locate the sentence in it that answers each question below. The student will read the answer and underline it.

Paragraph #1:
What are the names of the provinces located in the Atlantic Region? (*Prince Edward Island, New Brunswick, Newfoundland and Labrador, Nova Scotia*)

Paragraph #2:
What are the names of the four large islands found in this region? (*Prince Edward Island, Cape Breton Island, Newfoundland, Anticosti Island*)

Paragraph #3:
Which province in the Atlantic Region is flat and sandy? (*Prince Edward Island*)

Paragraph #4:
What is the major industry in the Atlantic Region? (*manufacturing*)
Why is fishing and fish processing no longer a major industry? (*the decline in the number of fish in the Grand Banks*)

Paragraph #5:
What is summer like in the Atlantic Region? (*mild, wet, foggy*)
What two things happen in Newfoundland and Labrador that the other provinces do not experience? (*icebergs floating in the ocean; 100 days of fog each year*)

Paragraph #6:
What are the names of the capital cities of the provinces in the Atlantic Region? (*P.E.I. - Charlottetown; NFLD and LAB - St. John's; N.B. Fredericton; N.S. - Halifax*)

B. Worksheets 1 to **5** found on **pages 70 to 74** are to be used as research and mapping activities reproduced for students. With the use of the Internet, reference books, atlases, and wall maps, students will find the missing information and will record it on the lines provided on the worksheets. Students may work independently, or in groups of two or four.

The Atlantic Provinces

Answer Key for Worksheet #1: Location and Land Surface page 70
Location: 1. peninsula; island; Cape Breton; Canso; Chignecto 2. a) Chaleur Bay b) Bay of Fundy c) Northumberland Strait d) Maine; Québec; Nova Scotia 3. smallest; Gulf of St. Lawrence; Northumberland Strait; bridge; 13.3 kilometres; Borden; Cape Tormentine
4. Atlantic Ocean; Gulf of St. Lawrence; Cabot Strait; island; mainland
Land Surface: 1.a) The Atlantic Uplands b) The Coastal Lowlands 2.a) Cobequid Mountains
b) Cape Breton Highlands 3. a) Annapolis-Cornwallis Valley 4. Appalachian; rugged; Lowland
5. Canadian Shield; Appalachian 6. a) Torngat Mountains b) Long Range Mountains
c) Mealey Mountains

Answer Key for Worksheet #2: Climate, Waterways, and Mineral Resources page 71
Climate: 1. Labrador 2. Nova Scotia 3. one; hundred 4. colder; warmer
Waterways: 1. isthmus 2. Bay of Fundy; Northumberland Strait 3. Labrador Current 4. Gulf Stream 5.a) Newfoundland and Labrador b) New Brunswick c) New Brunswick d) New Brunswick e) New Brunswick f) Newfoundland and Labrador g) Nova Scotia h) Nova Scotia
i) Prince Edward Island
Mineral Resources: 1. zinc, silver, lead, potash, coal, gypsum, salt, asbestos, gold, limestone, sand, gravel, tin, peat 2. Cape Breton Island 3. Grand Lake 4. Newfoundland and Labrador
5. Labrador City; Wabush on Newfoundland and Labrador's mainland

Answer Key for Worksheet #3: Agriculture and Fishing page 72
Agriculture: 1. The soil is not very fertile. 2. Prince Edward Island. 3.a) Subsistence farming
b) fruit farming c) potatoes, Prince Edward Island d) general farming e) apples f) fur farming
g) field crops h) dairy farming
Fishing: 1.a) continental shelf b) Grand Banks c) cod, Atlantic salmon d) coastline
e) trawler, dragger, fishing boat 2. lobster, shrimp, flounder, snow crab, scallops, herring

Answer Key for Worksheet #4: Cities in the Atlantic Provinces and Mapping Skills page 73
Cities in the Atlantic Provinces: 1. Charlottetown; East River; harbour; capital 2. Halifax; south; Canso; Sable; harbour; vessels 3. Fredericton; Saint John 4. Saint John; Saint John; Bay of Fundy; harbour 5. St. John's; Avalon; capital 6. Corner Brook; Grand Falls

Answer Key for Map of the Atlantic Provinces page 74
Waterways: 1. Strait of Belle Isle 2. Atlantic Ocean 3. Gulf of St. Lawrence 4. Cabot Strait
5. Strait of Canso 6. Bay of Fundy 7. Saint John River
Provinces: 1. New Brunswick 2. Nova Scotia 3. Prince Edward Island 4. Newfoundland
5. Labrador
Cities and Towns: 1. Edmundston 2. Fredericton 3. Saint John 4. Yarmouth 5. Lunenburg
6. Halifax 7. Dartmouth 8. Truro 9. Lunenburg 10. Borden 11. Charlottetown 12. Souris
13. Sydney 14. Corner Brook 15. Gander 16. Grand Falls 17. St. John's

The Atlantic Provinces

Information Sheet #1

The Atlantic Region is found on the east coast of Canada. It was the first area of Canada to be explored and settled. The Atlantic Region consists of four provinces: Newfoundland and Labrador, New Brunswick, Nova Scotia, and Prince Edward Island. The Gaspé and Anticosti Island are also part of this region. New Brunswick and Nova Scotia form part of Canada's mainland. Newfoundland and Labrador consists of the island and Labrador on the mainland. The Atlantic Region covers five percent of the total area of Canada, which is 540 303 square kilometres.

The Gulf of St. Lawrence is surrounded by the Atlantic Region. The Atlantic Ocean is found on its eastern and southern edge. No part of this region is far from the sea. Four large islands are found in the Atlantic Region. They are Newfoundland, Cape Breton Island, Anticosti Island, and Prince Edward Island. Nova Scotia and the Gaspé are peninsulas. A peninsula is an area of land almost completely surrounded by water.

Most of the Atlantic Region is made up of the Appalachian Region, which consists of low rolling hills, except for Prince Edward Island, which is flat and sandy, and Newfoundland and Labrador, which belongs to the Canadian Shield. The main farming areas in the region are in the Annapolis Lowlands, the Saint John River Valley, and Prince Edward Island, as most of the soil in the rest of the region is poor and not suited for agriculture.

Fish and fish processing were major industries in the Atlantic Region until the decline in the fish population on the Grand Banks and in other places of the Atlantic Ocean. The Grand Banks is an area of shallow water southeast of Newfoundland and Labrador. It was once the largest fishing grounds in the world. Other products, such as lobsters and scallops, are still fished from the ocean. New Brunswick and Prince Edward Island are famous for their potatoes. Apples are grown in the Annapolis Valley. Forestry and the manufacture of pulp and paper employ many people. Iron ore and coal are still mined in some areas. Manufacturing is now the leading industry. Tourism has grown rapidly as visitors enjoy the rustic beauty and scenery of the region and its quiet, peaceful charm.

During the winter, the coastal areas of the region experience snowy and stormy weather. During the summer it is mild, wet, and often foggy. Icebergs are often carried by the Labrador Current to the east coast of Newfoundland and Labrador and keep the air cool until the end of May. Newfoundland and Labrador average more than one hundred days of fog per year. Inland areas in New Brunswick and the Gaspé experience colder winters and warmer summers.

Only nine percent of Canada's people live in the Atlantic Provinces. The total population of the region is 2 327 638 (2011 statistics). More than half of the people live in cities and towns along the coasts. The three largest cities in the region are Halifax in Nova Scotia, Saint John in New Brunswick, and St. John's in Newfoundland and Labrador. Each Atlantic Province has a capital city. The capital cities are: St. John's, Newfoundland and Labrador; Charlottetown, Prince Edward Island; Fredericton, New Brunswick; and Halifax, Nova Scotia.

The Atlantic Provinces

Worksheet #1: Location and Land Surface

Location:

1. The province of **Nova Scotia** consists of two main parts - the mainland, which is a _____, and an _____ called _____ Island. The island is connected to the mainland by the _____ Causeway. The province of Nova Scotia is joined to the province of New Brunswick by the Isthmus of _____.

2. The province of **New Brunswick** has the following sea boundaries:
   a) north _____ b) south _____ c) east _____
   Its land boundary on the west side is the state of _____. To the north is _____ and to the south is _____.

3. **Prince Edward Island** is the _____ province in Canada. It is surrounded by water. To the northeast its water boundary is the _____ and to the west its water boundary is the _____. Today, Prince Edward Island is connected to the mainland of New Brunswick by a _____ that is _____ kilometres in length. It connects _____ on Prince Edward Island and _____ in New Brunswick.

4. Newfoundland and Labrador is bounded on the south, east ,and north by the _____ _____ and on the west by the _____ and _____. The province of Newfoundland and Labrador consists of an _____ and the _____ called Labrador.

Land Surface:

Use an atlas that has various types of maps to locate the answers to these activities.

1. Name two important landforms found in Nova Scotia.
   a) _____ b) _____

2. Name two low mountain ranges located in Nova Scotia.
   a) _____ b) _____

3. Name a famous fruit-growing valley found in Nova Scotia.
   a) _____

4. The greater part of New Brunswick consists of the _____ Mountains. These mountains are _____ hills that rise 300 to 800 metres above sea level. _____ areas are found along the coast.

5. Newfoundland and Labrador's mainland is covered with the _____ and its island consists of the _____ Mountains, which are mainly hills.

6. Name three mountain ranges found in Newfoundland and Labrador.
   a) _____ b) _____
   c) _____

SSJ192 ISBN 9781771586900

The Atlantic Provinces

Worksheet #2: Climate, Waterways, and Mineral Resources

Climate:

1. The cold _____ Current is responsible for extensive fog and clouds in the spring and the early summer along the coast of the Atlantic provinces.

2. The heaviest rainfall occurs along the outer coast of _____.

3. Newfoundland and Labrador averages more than _____ _____ days of fog a year.

4. New Brunswick's inland areas experience _____ winters and _____ summers.

Waterways:

1. The narrow strip of land connecting Nova Scotia to New Brunswick is called an _____.

2. This narrow strip of land separates two bodies of water called the _____ and the _____.

3. The cold ocean current coming from the north and making summers cooler in the Atlantic provinces is called the _____.

4. The warm ocean current coming from the south and making the winters not so cold is the _____.

5. In which Atlantic province is each of the following rivers located?
   a) Exploits River _____   f) Churchill River _____
   b) Petitcodiac River _____   g) Shubernacadie River _____
   c) Miramichi River _____   h) Annapolis River _____
   d) Saint John River _____   i) East River _____
   e) Kennebecasis River _____

Mineral Resources:

1. List the important minerals found in the Atlantic Provinces.

   _____

   _____

2. Where is coal mined in Nova Scotia?

   _____

3. The chief coal field in New Brunswick is situated near _____.

4. In which Atlantic province are there iron-ore mines? _____

5. Where are the iron-ore mines located?

   _____

   _____

The Atlantic Provinces

Worksheet #3: Agriculture and Fishing

Agriculture:

1. Why are the Atlantic Provinces, for the most part, not suitable for agriculture?

_____

2. Which Atlantic Province is the most suitable for agriculture?

_____

3. Choose words from the box to complete each sentence.

potatoes apples	Prince Edward Island subsistence farming	general farming dairy farming	fur farming field crops	fruit farming

a) _____ means a farmer only grows enough food for his own use and makes no profit from his land.

b) The Annapolis-Cornwallis Valley in Nova Scotia is the only large area used for _____ _____ in the Atlantic Provinces.

c) The main crop of the St. John Valley area in New Brunswick is _____. They are also grown extensively in _____.

d) When a farmer does not specialize in any crop but grows wheat, oats, or hay, or keeps cows, pigs, and poultry, the farming is called _____.

e) _____ are the main fruit grown in the Annapolis Valley.

f) _____ had its beginning in Prince Edward Island and is now found on the western shore of Nova Scotia.

g) Crops such as wheat, clover, hay, and oats are called _____.

h) One often finds _____ near large cities because of the good markets there.

Fishing:

1. Choose words from the box to complete the sentences.

continental shelf Atlantic salmon	cod trawler	Grand Banks dragger	fishing boat coastline

a) A _____ is part of a continent submerged beneath the sea.

b) The _____ is a large part of a continental shelf that lies off the coast of the Atlantic Provinces.

c) At one time, _____ and _____ were caught in the Grand Banks.

d) Fishing ports are numerous in the Atlantic Provinces because its _____ is indented.

e) If a fisher was going deep-sea fishing he would use a _____, a _____ or a _____.

2. Name six types of fish or seafood that are caught in the waters near the Atlantic Provinces.

_____

The Atlantic Provinces

Worksheet #4: Cities in the Atlantic Provinces and Mapping Skills

Cities in the Atlantic Provinces:

1. The most important and only city in Prince Edward Island is _____. It is situated on a bay which leads into the _____. Its founders decided that it was an excellence place to build a city because of its well-protected _____. It is the _____ city on Prince Edward Island.

2. The capital city of Nova Scotia is _____. It is situated on the _____ shore of Nova Scotia, about half-way between the Strait of _____ and Cape _____. It is known for its large natural _____ that is big enough for large ocean _____.

3. The capital of New Brunswick is _____, which is situated on the _____ River.

4. The largest and oldest city in New Brunswick is _____. It is located at the mouth of the _____ River where it empties into the _____ of _____. Like many other large cities in the Atlantic Provinces, its excellent _____ was a large factor in deciding its location.

5. The largest city in Newfoundland and Labrador is _____. It is found on the east coast of the _____ Peninsula. St. John's is one of the oldest cities of North America. It is also Newfoundland and Labrador's _____ city.

6. _____ and _____ have paper mills which supply much of the world's newsprint.

Mapping Skills:

On a map of the Atlantic Provinces, locate and label the following. The names of the waterways are to be printed in the boxes. The names of the provinces are to be printed on the double lines. The names of cities and towns are to be printed on the lines beside the dots.

a) **Waterways:** Atlantic Ocean; Gulf of St. Lawrence; Bay of Fundy; Cabot Strait; Strait of Canso; Strait of Belle Isle; Saint John River

b) **Provinces:** Newfoundland and Labrador; New Brunswick; Nova Scotia; Prince Edward Island

c) **Cities and Towns:** Fredericton; Charlottetown; Sydney; Moncton; Halifax; St. John's; Lunenburg; Souris; Cornerbrook; Edmundston; Truro; Saint John; Borden; Yarmouth; Grand Falls; Gander

Map of the Atlantic Provinces

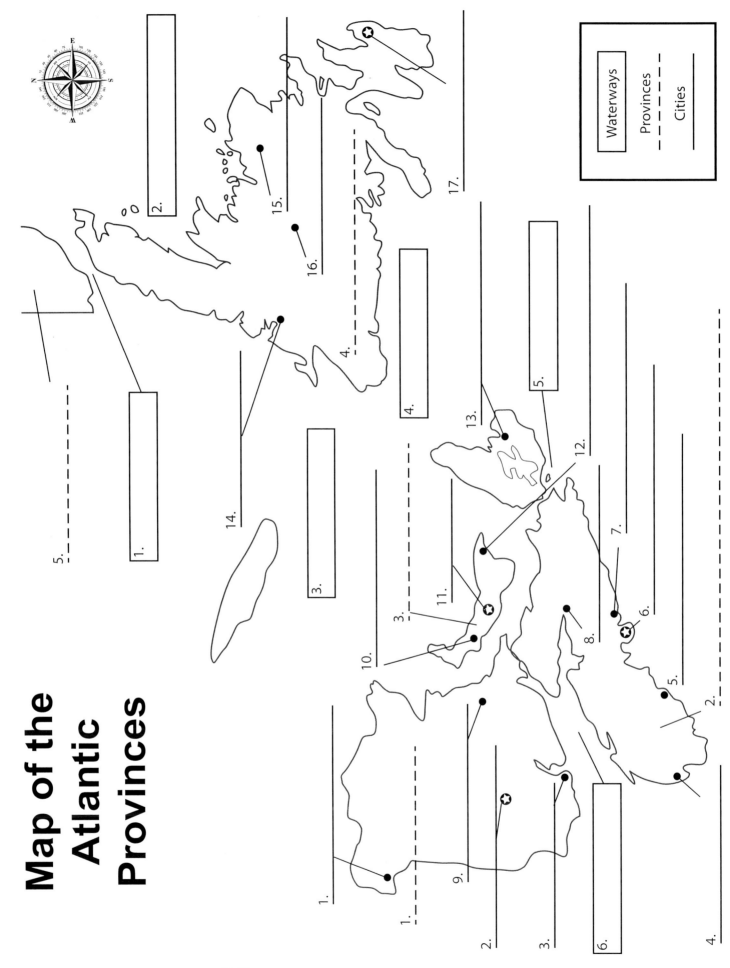

Waterways

Provinces

Cities

SSJ192   ISBN 9781771586900

© On The Mark Press

Québec

Lesson Plan #13: Québec

Expectations:

Students will
• become more knowledgeable and better acquainted with the location, physical features, climate, bodies of water, agriculture, mineral resources, industries, cities, symbols, and flag of Québec.
• develop reading and research skills to locate answers requested.
• identify and label a map of Québec.

A. Reproduce the information sheet called "Québec" for your students to read independently or display it on a white board for large group reading and discussion.

Brainstorm for facts that the students may already know about Québec. List them on a chart.

Have your students read the information in each paragraph. Then have a student locate the sentence in the paragraph that answers each question and underline it.

Paragraph #1: How does Québec compare in size to the other provinces in Canada? (*It is the largest.*) Why is Québec City such a famous city? (*It is the capital city of the province and the oldest one in Canada.*) Where does the word Québec come from? (*It is an Algonquin word "kebec."*) What does it mean? (*It means "the place where the river narrows."*) Who gave Québec City its name? (*Samuel de Champlain*) What did he build at Québec City? (*the first settlement in Canada*)

Paragraph #2: What is the population of Québec? (*7 903 001*) How does Québec rank in provincial population? (*the second highest*) Why is the province of Québec unique and different? (*Most of the people are French Canadian and speak French most of the time.*) Who else lives in Québec as well? (*people of British descent, aboriginal people, and immigrants*)

Paragraph #3 and #4: What are the four main land regions in Québec? (*Canadian Shield; St. Lawrence Lowlands; Appalachian Region; Hudson Bay Lowlands*) Have students locate the four regions on a Physical Features Map of Québec. Which physical region covers most of Québec? (*The Canadian Shield*) How much does it cover? (*nine-tenths*) What is the land like in this area? (*little or no soil; heavily forested; many lakes, rivers, streams*) Is farming carried out in this region? (*No*) What does this region have that can be used? (*minerals*) Where is this region found? (*It includes the North Shore which extends along the St. Lawrence from the Saguenay River to Labrador.*)

Paragraph #5: Where are the St. Lawrence Lowlands located? (*They are located along the St. Lawrence River Valley and the Montréal Plain.*) Why is farming carried on in this area? (*It has very fertile soil.*) What is produced in this area? (*dairy cattle, hogs, milk, maple syrup*) Why do you think this area is so heavily populated? (*Answers will vary.*)

Paragraph #6: Where is the Appalachian Region in Québec? (*It extends from Vermont along the provinces southeastern boundary to the Gaspé Peninsula.*) Describe the terrain in this area. (*heavily forested; mountainous; many lakes and streams*) Where are the Hudson Bay Lowlands located? (*a small strip of land south of James Bay*)

Québec

Paragraph #7: What is Québec's climate like? (*winters are long and cold; summers are warm but short*) What does Québec receive often? (*a lot of snow*)

Paragraph #8 and Paragraph #9: What are the main industries in Québec? (*manufacturing goods; producing hydro-electric power, raw materials, paper*) Why is Québec a leader in paper production? (*It has many forests.*) Why is it a leader in the production of electricity? (*It has large amounts of water power.*) What industry is growing in Québec? (*tourism*) Why would Québec attract tourists? (*It has an interesting history; mountains for skiing; lakes for fishing; camping; famous cities*)

B. Worksheets #1 to #4 found on pages 79 to 82 are to be used as research activities and reproduced for students. With the use of the Internet, reference books, atlases, and wall maps, students will record the answers on the lines provided. Students may work independently, or in groups of two or four.

Answer Key for Worksheet #1: Location, Surface, Climate, and Rivers of Québec page 79
Location:
northeastern; Ontario; Labrador; New Brunswick; Maine; New York; Hudson; largest

Surface:
St. Lawrence Lowlands; Appalachian Highlands; Canadian Shield; Hudson Bay Lowlands; narrow; band; fertile; Ninety; mountain; range; Laurentian Plateau; James Bay

Climate: varies; long; cold; 120; 160; precipatation; temperatures; hot; humid

Rivers of Québec:
1. Ottawa River 2. St. Maurice River, Ottawa River, Saguenay River, Manicouagon River
3. Harricana River, Nottaway River; George River, Rivière-a-la-Baleine, Koksoak River, Rivière aux Feuilles, 4. Rivière-de-Rupert, Eastmain River, Openaca River, Old Factory River, Fort George River, Roggan River, Grand Rivière-de-la-Baleine, Broadback River 5. Lac St. Jean
6. Lake Minto 7. James Bay 8. Richelieu River, Chaudière River, St. Frances River

Answer Key for Worksheet #2: Agriculture and Industries of Québec page 80

Agriculture:
1. dairy; 40 000; St. Lawrence River; half; butter; cheese 2. oats, barley, wheat, corn 3. apples, blueberries, raspberries, strawberries 4. cabbages, carrots, lettuce, peas, sweet corn, tomatoes, potatoes 5. hogs, poultry, beef cattle 6. maple sugar, maple syrup, sap

Industries:
1. farming, mining, manufacturing, hydro-electric power, technology, forestry, pulp and paper, electricity 2. pulp and paper, electricity 3. aerospace industry 4. Noranda 5. Schefferville
6. Noranda, Val d'Or 7. asbestos, titanium

Answer Key for Worksheet #3: Québec's Cities and Mapping Skills page 81
1. Québec City; walled; oldest; Samuel de Champlain; port; tourist 2. Montréal; island; popular 3. Trois Rivières; halfway 4. Gaspé; Sherbrooke; Rouyn; Rimouski; Sept Iles; Rivière-du-Loup; Val d'Or; Hull

Québec

Answer Key for Map of Québec Page 82

Waterways: 1. Hudson Strait 2. Ungava Bay 3. Strait of Belle Isle 4. Strait of Jacques Cartier 5. Strait of Honguedo 6. St. Lawrence River 7. Ottawa River 8. James Bay 9. Hudson Bay

Provinces:
1. Ontario 2. Québec 3. Newfoundland and Labrador 4. New Brunswick

Cities and Towns:
1. Sept Isles 2. Gaspé 3. Rimouski 4. Rivière du Loup 5. Sherbrooke 6. Hull 7. Montréal 8. Trois Rivières 9. Québec City 10. Rouyn 11. Val d'Or

Québec

Information Sheet

Québec is the largest province in Canada, covering 1 540 630 square kilometres. Québec City is the province's capital city. It is the oldest city in Canada. Montréal is the largest city in Québec and one of the busiest. The word Québec comes from the Algonquin word "kebec," which means "the place where the river narrows." The French explorer, Samuel de Champlain, heard the native people use this word to describe a place on the St. Lawrence River. It is at this place where he built a settlement and founded Québec City in 1608. It was the first permanent settlement in Canada.

The province of Québec ranks the second highest in population next to Ontario. There are 7 237 479 people (2011 census) living in Québec. Eighty percent of the people in Québec are French Canadian and speak French. The strong French influence makes Québec unique and quite different from the rest of the provinces and territories. Many of the people are Roman Catholic. Most children are instructed in French and receive instruction pertaining to religion. Ten percent of the people are of British descent. A large number of First Nations People live in northern Québec as well.

Québec has four main land regions: The Canadian Shield; The St. Lawrence Lowlands; The Appalachian Region; and The Hudson Bay Lowlands.

The Canadian Shield covers nine-tenths of the province. It includes the North Shore, which extends along the St. Lawrence River from the Saguenay River to Labrador. Most of the ancient rocks in this region have little or no soil at all. This area is a wilderness of forests, lakes, rivers, and streams. This region has little land that can be farmed but it does have a variety of mineral deposits.

The St. Lawrence Lowlands consists of the St. Lawrence River Valley and the Montréal Plain. The lowlands are about sixteen kilometres wide near Québec City and broaden to one hundred kilometres at Montréal. The fertile soil in this valley supports most of Québec's farming. Québec is a leading producer of dairy cattle, hogs, milk, and maple syrup. This area is one of the most heavily populated regions of Canada.

The Appalachian Region extends from Vermont along the province's southeastern boundary to the Gaspé Peninsula. This area is heavily forested, mountainous, and dotted with lakes and streams. The Hudson Bay Lowlands extends into Québec from Ontario. It covers a small strip of land south of James Bay.

Québec's coastline is 13 773 kilometres long and includes bays, inlets, and offshore islands. The main bodies of water that surround it are: James Bay and Hudson Bay on the west, Hudson Strait and Ungava Bay on the north, and the Gulf of St. Lawrence on the southeast and south.

The climate in Québec varies greatly. Its winters are long and cold, and its summers are warm but short. During the winter, southern Québec can receive 246 to 442 centimetres of snow between November and mid-March.

Québec is a leading manufacturer and produces about a fourth of all the goods manufactured in Canada. Most of the paper in North America is produced in Québec due to its abundant forests. It is a leader in the production of hydro-electric power due to its abundant supply of water power. Québec's natural resources provide many of its industries with valuable raw materials. Québec's rich history, rugged terrain, beautiful lakes, and rolling farmland attract tourists and outdoor enthusiasts yearly. Tourism is a growing trade in Québec.

Québec

Worksheet #1: Location, Surface, Climate, and Rivers of Québec

Location:

Québec is a large triangle of land found in the _____ corner of North America. It is bordered by _____ to the west; _____ to the east; the state of _____ and _____ State to the south; and the _____ Strait to the north. It is the _____ province in Canada.

Surface:

Québec has four main regions. They are the _____, the _____, the _____, and the _____. The St. Lawrence Lowlands is a _____ _____ of land along the St. Lawrence River. This area contains the province's most _____ land. _____ percent of the people of this province live here. The Appalachian Highlands are a low _____ _____ that lies between the St. Lawrence River and the American Border. The Canadian Shield Region is also known as the _____. It covers ninety percent of Québec. The Hudson Bay Lowlands cover a small strip of land south of _____.

Climate:

Québec's climate _____ greatly. Its winters are _____ and _____. A winter can last for _____ to _____ days. The cold winds from the North Pole collide with warm winds from the south causing much _____ and varied _____. In the southern part of Québec summers can be _____ and _____.

Rivers:

Using an atlas or a large map of the province of Québec, locate the following rivers found in Québec.

1. The river that forms part of the boundary between Ontario and Québec is the _____
_____.

2. The four chief tributaries of the St. Lawrence River are _____,
_____, _____, and _____.

3. Six rivers that flow north are the _____, _____,
_____, _____, _____, and the _____.

4. Four rivers flowing west are _____, _____,
_____, and _____.

5. The Saguenay River starts from _____.

6. The source of the Red Leaf River (Rivière aux Feuilles) is _____.

7. The body of water into which the Fort George River empties is _____.

8. A southern tributary of the St. Lawrence River is _____.

SSJ192 ISBN 9781771586900

Québec

Worksheet #2: Agriculture and Industries of Québec

Agriculture:

1. Québec is one of the great agricultural provinces of Canada and is known for its
_____ farming. There are more than _____ farms in Québec, mainly
along the _____, and over _____ of them are dairy farms. They
supply milk for the making of _____ and _____.

2. Name four types of grains grown in Québec.

_____, _____, _____ , _____

3. What types of fruits are grown on Québec's farms?

_____, _____, _____ , _____

4. What types of vegetables are grown on Québec's farms?

_____, _____, _____ , _____

_____, _____, _____

5. Québec farmers also raise _____, _____, and

_____.

6. Québec is famous all over the world for its _____ _____ and _____
_____, which are made from the _____ of maple trees.

Québec's Industries:

1. List eight major industries found in the province of Québec.

_____   _____

_____   _____

_____   _____

_____   _____

2. The main industry in Québec is the production of _____. It is also the largest
producer of _____ in Canada.

3. Québec has the fifth largest _____ _____ in the world.

4. The world's largest copper smelter is located in _____.

5. Iron ore is mined at _____ and along the Québec-Labrador border.

6. Gold is mined at _____ and _____.

7. Québec is the leading producer of _____. It produces all of Canada's
_____, which is used in paint.

Québec

Worksheet #3: Québec's Cities and Mapping Skills

Québec's Cities:

1. _____ _____ is the capital city of the Province of Québec. It is the only _____ city in North America and the _____ city in Canada. It was founded by a famous French explorer named _____ in 1608. It is an important _____ and _____ attraction.

2. _____ is the largest city in Québec. It is located on an _____ in the St. Lawrence River. It is a _____ tourist attraction for visitors.

3. _____ _____ is known as "paper town" as it produces ten percent of the world's paper. It is located on the St. Lawrence River _____ between Montréal and Québec City.

4. Explore a map of the province of Québec and locate the names of eight other cities and towns.

_____   _____

_____   _____

_____   _____

_____   _____

Map Work:

Follow the following steps:

On a map of the province of Québec locate the following places.

     1. The names of the waterways are to be printed in the boxes.

     2. The names of provinces are to be printed in the ovals.

     3. The names of cities and towns are to be printed on the lines beside the dots.

a) **Waterways:**

St. Lawrence River; Ungava Bay; Hudson Strait; Ottawa River; Strait of Honguedo; James Bay Strait of Jacques Cartier; Strait of Belle Isle; Hudson Bay

b) **Cities and Towns:**

Québec City; Sherbrooke; Sept-Iles; Rouyn; Gaspé; Hull; Rimouski; Val d'or; Montréal; Trois Riviéres; Riviére du Loup

c) **Provinces:**

New Brunswick; Ontario; Newfoundland and Labrador; Québec

Map of Québec

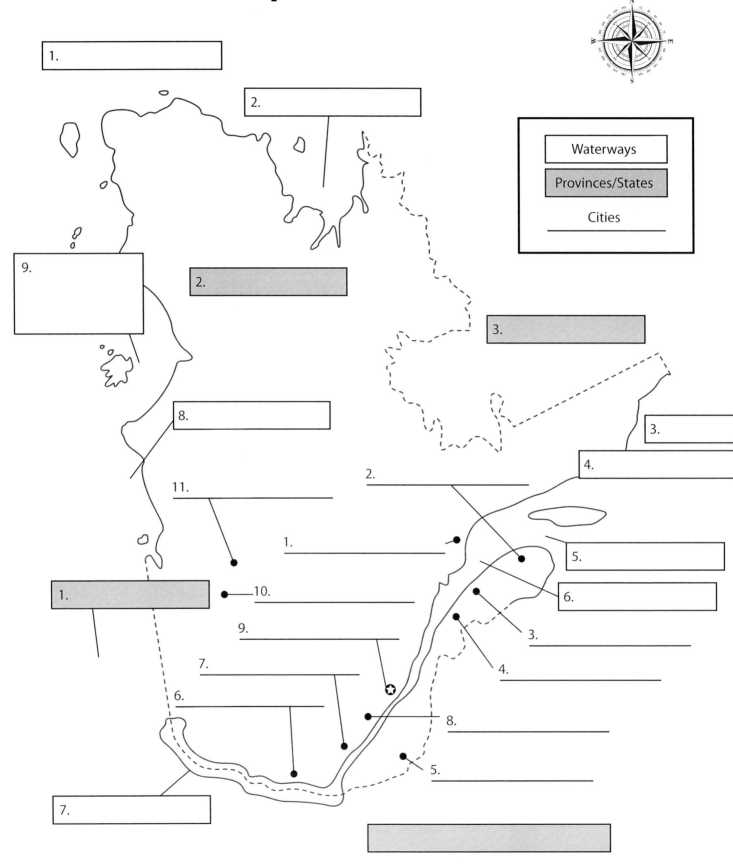

Waterways

Provinces/States

Cities

1.

2.

2.

3.

9.

3.

4.

8.

2.

11.

1.

5.

1.

10.

6.

9.

3.

7.

4.

6.

8.

7.

5.

SSJ192 ISBN 9781771586900

© On The Mark Press

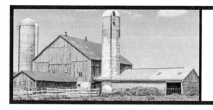
Ontario

Lesson Plan 14: Ontario

Expectations:

Students will:

- become more knowledgeable and better acquainted with the location, physical features, climate, bodies of water, boundaries, agriculture, mineral resources, industries, cities, symbols and flag of Ontario.
- develop reading and research skills by locating answers requested.
- identify and label maps of Ontario.

A. Reproduce the **"Information Sheets #1"** called **"Ontario"** found on **pages 86 to 87** for your students to read independently or display them on a white board for large group reading and discussion. Brainstorm for facts the students already know about Ontario. Have your students read the information in each paragraph. Then have a student locate the sentence in the paragraph that answers each question and read it aloud.

Paragraph #1:

How big is Ontario? (*second largest provice in area*) Who gave Ontario its name? (*the Iroquois aboriginal people*) What does Ontario mean? (*beautiful lake, rocks standing high, near the water*) What was Ontario named after? (*Niagara Falls*) What is Ontario's capital city? (*Toronto*) Why is Toronto such an important city? (*It is the busiest port on the Great Lakes.*) What other capital city is located in Ontario? (*Ottawa*) Where is Ottawa located? (*on the Ottawa River*)

Paragraph #2:

What is Ontario's population? (*12 851 821*) Why is this important? (*It has the largest population of all the provinces.*) Where do most of the people live in Ontario? (*southernmost part near the Great Lakes and large cities*) What else does Ontario have more of than the other provinces in Canada? (*large cities*) Describe the population in Ontario. (*made up of people from all over the world*)

Paragraph #3 to #4:

What are the four main land regions in Ontario? (*Hudson Bay Lowlands, Canadian Shield, St. Lawrence Lowlands, Great Lakes Lowlands*) Describe the Hudson Bay Lowlands. (*flat, poorly drained, muskegs or peat bogs in northern areas; permafrost – permanently frozen ground*) Where is this region located? (*They curve around the southern part of the Hudson Bay and extend as far south as Kesagami Lake.*) Have a student point to this area on a large wall map.

Paragraph #5:

What is the name of another land region in Ontario? (*Canadian Shield*) Where is it located? (*below the Hudson Bay Lowlands and stretches to a narrow area along Lake Ontario*) Have a student locate this region on a large wall map. Describe this region. (*many small lakes and rivers, forests, wild animals, minerals, timber, clay belt for growing crops, and grassland for beef cattle and dairy cattle*)

 # Ontario

Paragraph #6:
Where would you find the St. Lawrence Lowlands? (*along the St. Lawrence River*) Have a student locate it on a wall map. Describe this area. (*wedge-shaped; located between Ottawa and the St. Lawrence River; low hills; fertile valleys; able to grow many things*)

Paragraph #7: Where are the Great Lakes Lowlands located? (*This area touches the lakes Erie, Huron, St. Clair, and Ontario.*) Have a student locate this area on a wall map. Describe this area. (*fertile soil, land is flat, protected by an escarpment*) What grows well in this area? (*fruit*)

Paragraph #8 and #9:
How long is Ontario's inland shoreline? (*8 452 kilometres*) What does it stretch around? (*Lakes of Erie, Ontario, Huron, Superior*) What is the name of the largest inland island in the world? (*Manitoulin Island*) In which Great Lake is it found? (*Lake Huron*) How is the province of Ontario rich? (*It is filled with many streams, rivers, waterfalls; has a natural water highway for large boats into the interior of Canada; Niagara River and other rivers are able to supply abundant electric power*)

Paragraph #10:
Describe Ontario's climate. (*milder in southern Ontario; winds from the Great Lakes make its climate warmer; colder in northern Ontario; cold winds come from the Arctic or the Prairies; temperature and snowfall vary during the seasons; summers are warmer in southern Ontario*)

Paragraph #11 to #14:
What is the most important industry in Ontario? (*manufacturing*) Which city is a leader in manufacturing? (*Toronto*) What do the main industries produce? (*vehicles, chemicals, food, beverages, electrical products, metal products, paper products, printed materials*) Which industry produces a third of Canada's mineral products? (*mining*) What are the names of important mining centres in Ontario? (*Sudbury, Cochrane, Kenora, Thunder Bay*) Where is electricity produced in Ontario?(*nuclear power plants, fuel-burning power plants, hydro-electric plants*) Why do you think Ontario is called the industrial heartland of Canada? (*Answers may vary.*)

B. Worksheets #1 - #5 found on **pages 88 to 94** are to be used as research activities and reproduced for students to complete. With the use of the internet, reference books, atlases, and wall maps, students will record the answers on the lines provided. Students may work independently or in groups of two or groups of four. The missing words for each section could also be posted on a white board for the students to use.

Answer Key for Worksheet #1: Location and Surface page 88
Location: 1. Hudson Bay, James Bay, Québec, Great Lakes, United States, Manitoba 2. half
3. Lake Michigan 4. Point Pelee 5. They use the St. Lawrence Seaway to get to the Great Lakes

Surface: 1. four; The Hudson Bay Lowlands; The Canadian Shield; The St. Lawrence Lowlands; The Great Lakes Lowlands 2. Hudson Bay; James Bay; flat; drained; muskegs; permafrost
3. horseshoe; rocky; lakes; forested; clay; grains; vegetables; beef; dairy cattle; grasslands; minerals; timber; game animals 4. St. Lawrence River; small; rich; dairy 5. Great Lakes: Erie; Huron; Ontario; fertile; crops; Beef; dairy 6. Niagara Escarpment; cliff; ridge; Manitoulin Island; Bruce Peninsula; natural; shelter; largest

Ontario

Answer Key for Mapping Activity #1 : Map of Ontario's Boundaries page 89
Map of Ontario's Boundaries: 1. Québec 2. Ottawa River 3. St. Lawrence River 4. Lake Ontario 5. Lake Erie 6. Lake St. Clair 7. Lake Huron 8. The United States 9. Lake Superior 10. Ontario 11. James Bay 12. Hudson Bay 13. Manitoba

Answer Key for Worksheet #2: Climate and Lakes and Rivers of Ontario page 90
Climate: 1. winter; spring; summer; autumn 2. Southern; milder; Northern; winds; colder 3. -5°C; -25°C; 12°C; 21°C; 4. 500 millimetres; twice

Lake and Rivers of Ontario:
1. Lake Superior 2. Lake St. Clair 3. Lake Ontario 4. Lake of the Woods; Rainy Lake; 5. St. Clair River 6. Niagara River 7. Abitibi River 8. Ottawa River 9. St. Mary's River 10. Madawaska River 11. Detroit River 12. Severn River

Answer Key for Worksheet #3: Agriculture and Forestry page 91
Agriculture:
1. biggest; livestock; corn 2. Dairy; milk; cheese; yoghurt; cream; ice cream; butter 3. meat; eggs 4. Niagara; peaches; cherries; plums; pears; grapes; wineries 5. marshes; vegetables; Holland Marsh; Thedford Marsh; Erieau Marsh; Pelee

Forestry:
1. government; licences; harvest 2. lumber; pulp; paper; twenty; northern; rivers; Huron; Superior, Nipissing; Veneer; Sault Ste Marie; Thessalon; Plywood; Cochrane; Hearst; New Liskeard; Kirkland Lake; Sturgeon Falls 3. a) coniferous b) deciduous 4.a) Barges carry the logs to the mills wherever there are no roads. b) The logs float in log booms until they are used.

Answer Key for Worksheet #4: Mining and Industries page 92
Mining: 1. minerals 2. nickel, cobalt, zinc, copper, gold, cement, platinum, silver, salt 3. a) nickel b) copper 4. nickel 5. zinc 6. gold

Industries:
1. • located near main cities and waterways in North America. • close to the United States and its large cities for trading purposes. • ocean-going vessels can visit many ports in Ontario.
2. The area from Toronto to the Niagara River is called the "Golden Horseshoe."
3. Hamilton, Sault Ste Marie 4. automobile; parts 5. Chemical 6. processing; foods; beverages; beer; soft drinks; liquor; fruits; vegetables; milk; dairy; mills; wheat; flour; grains; cereals

Answer Key for Worksheet #5: Cities and Towns in Ontario; Mapping Skills page 93
Ontario's Cities and Towns:
1. Pickering 2. Toronto; Hamilton; Sault Ste. Marie; Thunder Bay 3. Sudbury 4. Toronto; Peterborough 5. Oshawa; Windsor; Cambridge; Alliston; Oakville 6. Niagara Falls 7. Toronto; Ottawa; London; Kingston; Peterborough; Kitchener-Waterloo; Hamilton; Guelph; Oshawa 8. Hamilton, Sault Ste. Marie 9. Toronto 10. Ottawa

Answer Key for Mapping Activity #2 : Map of Ontario page 94
1. Thunder Bay 2. Sault Ste. Marie 3. Windsor 4. London 5. Niagara Falls 6. Hamilton 7. Toronto 8. Kingston 9. Ottawa 10. Pembroke 11. North Bay 12. Sudbury 13. Kirkland Lake 14. Timmins 15. Moose Factory

 # Ontario

Information Sheet #1

Of all the provinces in Canada, Ontario is the second largest in area. It covers 1 068 580 square kilometres of our country. It is the southernmost province, but it also extends so far north that some of its ground beneath the surface is permafrost (permanently frozen). Ontario's name comes from the Iroquois Aboriginal People. It may mean "beautiful lake" or "rocks standing high" or "near the water," which refer to Niagara Falls. Ontario's capital city is Toronto, which lies on the northwest shore of Lake Ontario. It is one of the busiest Canadian ports on the Great Lakes. Ottawa, the capital city of Canada, is also found in Ontario and is located on the Ottawa River.

Ontario has the largest population of all the provinces: 12 851 821 (2011 census). Most of the people live in 12 percent of the province's land area. Ontario is heavily populated mainly in the southernmost part near the Great Lakes and the larger cities. Ontario has 38 cities with a population of 50 000 or more. No other Canadian province has so many large cities. Ontario's population has become very multicultural and consists of people from all over the world.

Ontario has four main land regions. They are the Hudson Bay Lowlands, the Canadian Shield, the St. Lawrence Lowlands, and the Great Lakes Lowlands. The Hudson Bay Lowlands curve around the southern part of Hudson Bay and extend as far south as Kesagami Lake. This region is flat and poorly drained and large muskegs (peat bogs) are located in it. A narrow belt of permafrost (permanently frozen ground) is found in this lowland near the Arctic.

The Canadian Shield, a low rocky region, covers more than half of Ontario. The Canadian Shield is located below the Hudson Bay Lowlands and stretches to a narrow area along Lake Ontario. This region is filled with many small lakes and rivers surrounded by forests. The Canadian Shield is rich in gamelife, minerals, and timber. A large area called the clay belt, which extends from Hearst to the Québec border, supports a variety of crops grown by farmers and provides grassland for grazing beef and dairy cattle.

The St. Lawrence Lowlands runs along the St. Lawrence River. It is a wedge-shaped area located between the Ottawa and St. Lawrence Rivers. It contains low hills and fertile valleys. Fruits, grains, and vegetables are grown here, and dairy cattle are raised extensively.

The Great Lakes Lowlands lie along much of the Great Lakes in Ontario. It touches the Lakes of Erie, Huron, St. Clair, and Ontario. The soil here is very fertile and in many areas the land is flat. The Niagara Escarpment is a high cliff or ridge that extends 725 kilometres from Manitoulin Island through the Bruce Peninsula to Niagara Falls. The escarpment forms a shelter for Ontario's best fruit-growing belt.

Ontario's inland shoreline stretches 8 452 kilometres along the many bays, inlets, and sandy beaches of the Lakes of Erie, Ontario, Huron, and Superior. Manitoulin Island, found in Lake Huron, is the largest inland island in the world. It has an area of 2 765 square kilometres.

Ontario

Information Sheet #2

Ontario has over 400 000 lakes, countless streams, rivers, and waterfalls sprinkled throughout the province. The St. Lawrence River and the Great Lakes provide a natural highway for many ocean-going vessels into the interior of Canada. Hydro-electric plants on the Niagara River and other rivers provide Ontario with an abundant source of electric power.

Southern Ontario has a milder climate than the rest of the province. Winds from the Great Lakes moderate its climate. Northern Ontario experiences cold air waves from the Arctic or the Prairies. During the winter, the temperature and the amount of snow fall vary throughout the season. The summers are warmer in Southern Ontario than in Northern Ontario.

Ontario is known as the industrial heartland of Canada. Ontario's manufacturing industries make it one of the richest economic regions of North America. Industrial workers produce half of the country's manufactured products. Toronto is Canada's leading industrial centre. Major manufacturing industries produce vehicles, chemicals, food and beverages, electrical products, metal products, paper products, and printed materials.

Agriculture is an important industry in Ontario. There are approximately 68 000 farms in the province which use five percent of the land area and each farm is an average of 80 hectares in size. Ontario is the leading producer of fruits and vegetables, especially in the famous Niagara fruit belt. Beef and dairy farming produce many products sold throughout the province and Canada.

Mining in Ontario produces more than a third of Canada's most valuable mineral products. Sudbury, Cochran, Kenora, and Thunder Bay are important mining centres.

Electricity is produced in Ontario's nuclear power plants, fuel-burning power plants, and hydro-electric plants. Ontario Hydro, which operates many hydro-electric plants, is a large publicly-owned utility.

Rideau Canal

Parliament Buildings

CN Tower

SSJ192 ISBN 9781771586900 87

Ontario

Worksheet #1: Location and Surface

Location:

1. Name the boundaries of Ontario. Begin at the north-east and proceed in a clock-wise direction.

   _____

   _____

2. Approximately how much of the boundaries are water? _____

3. Which of the Great Lakes is not a boundary of Ontario? _____

4. What is the most southerly point of Ontario? _____

5. Although Ontario is an inland province, why are ocean vessels able to travel to its main cities?

   _____

   _____

6. On the accompanying map, mark on and name the boundaries of Ontario. Trace the boundary lines in red.

Surface:

1. Ontario has _____ main geographic regions. They are: _____

   _____

2. The Hudson Bay Lowlands curve around the southern part of _____ and
   _____. This area is _____, poorly _____ and has large
   _____ (peat bogs). In some areas there is _____ (permanently
   frozen land).

3. The Canadian Shield is a very large _____-shaped region that covers most of
   Ontario. It is a _____ region containing many _____ and
   _____ areas. Large rich _____ areas allow farmers to raise a
   variety of crops such as _____ and _____. Farmers are able to raise
   _____ and _____ _____ also on the _____.
   This area is also rich in _____, _____, and _____.

4. The St. Lawrence Lowlands runs along the _____.
   It is a _____ area wedged between the Ottawa and the St. Lawrence Rivers. The
   soil is _____ and farmers grow fruits and vegetables and large _____
   farms are found there.

5. The Great Lakes Lowlands lie along much of the _____ _____ in Canada. This
   region touches the lakes of _____, _____, and _____. The
   grey-brown soil is very _____ and many different kinds of _____ are
   grown. _____ and _____ cattle are also raised.

6. The _____ _____ is found in this region. It is a high _____ or
   _____ that runs for 725 kilometres from _____ _____
   through the _____ _____to Niagara Falls. This escarpment is
   a _____ _____ for Ontario's best fruit growing area. Canada's
   _____ cities are found in the Great Lakes Lowlands.

Map of Ontario's Boundaries

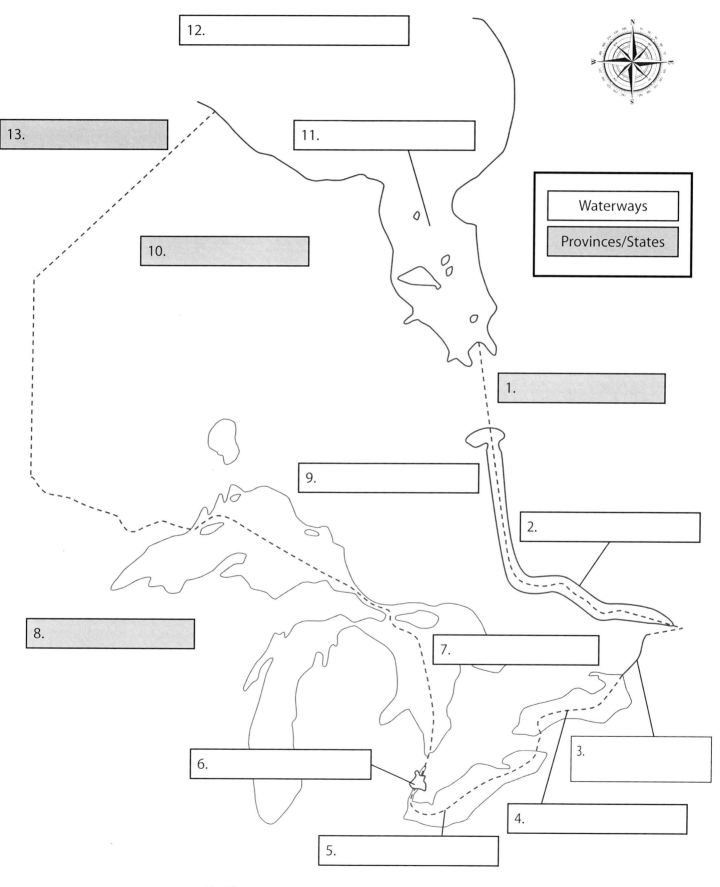

12.

13.

11.

Waterways

Provinces/States

10.

1.

9.

2.

8.

7.

6.

3.

4.

5.

SSJ192   ISBN 9781771586900

Ontario

Worksheet #2: Climate and Lakes and Rivers of Ontario

Climate:

1. All of Ontario has four distinct seasons. They are _____, _____, _____, and _____.

2. _____ Ontario has a much _____ climate than _____ Ontario due to the _____ from the Great Lakes. Northern Ontario is usually _____ in all the seasons.

3. The average winter temperature can range from _____ in Southern Ontario to _____ in Northern Ontario. The average midsummer temperature can be _____ in the province's far north and _____ in its southern areas.

4. The average rainfall for the province is _____ per year. Some parts of Southern Ontario receive _____ that much. Some areas in Northern Ontario receive up to 300 centimetres of snow a year.

Lakes and Rivers of Ontario:

Underline the correct answers:

1. The largest lake in or bordering Ontario is (Lake Nipigon, Lake Superior, Lake Simcoe, Lake Huron).

2. The smallest lake of the following group is (Lake Erie, Lake Nipigon, Lake Ontario, Lake St. Clair)

3. Lake (Huron, Nipissing, Ontario) flows directly into the St. Lawrence River.

4. An ocean vessel cannot enter (Lake Ontario, Lake of the Woods, Rainy Lake, Lake Superior).

5. The (Ottawa River, St. Clair River, Albany River) joins Lake St. Clair and Lake Huron.

6. The (St. Lawrence River, Niagara River, French River) joins Lake Ontario with Lake Erie.

7. The (Abitibi River, Nipigon River, Detroit River) flows into James Bay.

8. The (Rainy River, Ottawa River, Thames River) flows into the St. Lawrence River.

9. The (St. Mary's River, Trent River, Humber River) joins Lake Huron with Lake Superior.

10. The (Grand River, Madawaska River, Severn River) flows into the Ottawa River.

11. The (Rideau River, Detroit River, Nelson River) joins Lake St. Clair with Lake Erie.

12. The (Rainy River, Thames River, Severn River) flows north into Hudson Bay.

Ontario

Worksheet #3: Agriculture and Forestry

Agriculture:

1. Ontario is Canada's _____ agricultural producer. In Ontario, crops such as hay, oats, mixed grains, and corn are grown by farmers to feed their _____. In southern Ontario, _____ is the main crop grown.

2. _____ farming produces many products such as _____, _____, _____, _____, _____, and _____.

3. The raising of livestock for _____ and _____ has increased in Ontario.

4. Specialty farms are found in the _____ region. This area is famous for its _____, _____, _____, _____, _____, and other fruit. Many _____ have developed in this growing area.

5. Four _____ in Southern Ontario were drained so _____ could be grown. They are the _____, _____, _____, and the _____ Marshes. Some farmers use very large greenhouses to grow plants and vegetables in as well.

Forestry:

1. In Ontario, the _____ owns almost all of the forest land. The government sells _____ to private companies to _____ areas of forest.

2. Trees that are cut are used for _____ and to make _____ and _____. There are about _____ pulp and paper mills located in Ontario and most are found in the _____ part. The mills are located near major _____ and near large bodies of water such as Lake _____, _____, and _____. _____, a thin layer of wood made from hardwood trees, is manufactured in _____ and _____. _____, a type of board made of pressed veneer sheets, is manufactured in _____ and _____. Particle board is made at mills in _____, _____ and _____.

3. Name two kinds of forests found in Ontario.
   a) _____   b) _____

4. Give two reasons why waterways are important in the lumbering industry.
   a) _____
   _____
   b) _____
   _____

SSJ192 ISBN 9781771586900

Ontario

Worksheet #4: Mining and Industries

Mining:

1. The Canadian Shield is very rich in _____.

2. Name nine minerals that are found in Ontario.

_____   _____   _____

_____   _____   _____

_____   _____   _____

3. Name the two main minerals produced in Ontario.

a) _____   b) _____

4. What mineral is produced in Sudbury, Ontario? _____

5. What mineral is produced at Timmins? _____

6. Which valuable mineral is mined at Timmins, Kirkland Lake, and Red Lake? _____

Industries:

1. Tell why Ontario has become a great industrial province.

_____

_____

_____

_____

_____

_____

2. Where is the most important industrial area in Ontario?

_____

_____

3. Steel-making has been a leading industry in Ontario for a long time. Steel-making takes place in _____ and _____.

4. The _____ industry provides many Ontarians with work. Many factories make _____ for cars and trucks.

5. _____ production is the second highest manufacturing activity in Ontario.

6. The _____ of _____ and _____ is the third highest manufacturing industry in Ontario. _____, _____, and _____ are the leading beverages produced. Food plants process _____, _____, _____, and _____ products. Ontario _____ process _____ into _____, and other _____ are used for _____.

 # Ontario

Worksheet #5: Cities and Towns in Ontario; Mapping Skills

Cities and Towns:

Name the centre in Ontario where each of these industries take place.

1. It is the centre of atomic energy. _____

2. They are the four main important lake ports. _____

_____

3. It has a nickel refinery. _____

4. They are two cities that manufacture breakfast foods. _____

_____

5. There are five cities that manufacture cars in Ontario. Name them. _____

_____

6. It is an important hydro-electric centre. _____

7. There are nine cities that have universities. They are _____

_____

8. These two cities are steel-making centres. _____

9. It is home to the provincial government. _____

10. It is the centre where the federal government is held. _____

Mapping Activity:

On the map of Ontario, locate and neatly label the following cities.

Hamilton	Niagara Falls	Sudbury	Kingston
North Bay	Timmins	Kirkland Lake	Ottawa
Thunder Bay	London	Pembroke	Timmins
Moose Factory	Sault Ste. Marie	Toronto	

Map of Ontario

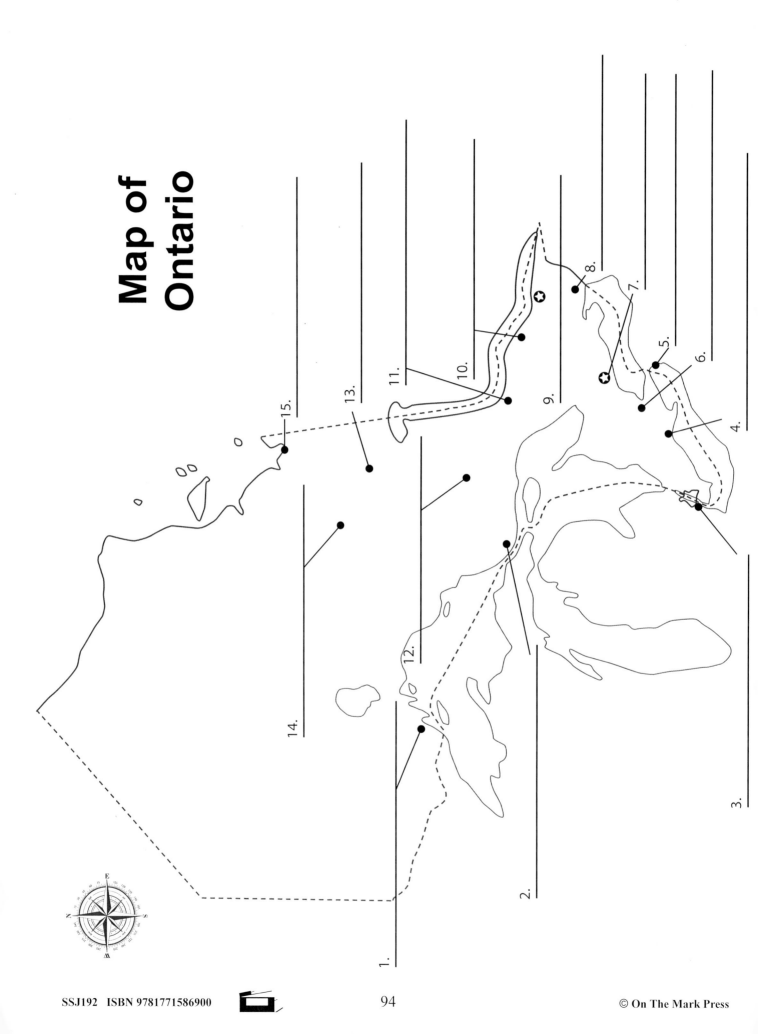

SSJ192   ISBN 9781771586900

Prairie Provinces

Lesson Plan 15: Manitoba, Saskatchewan, and Alberta

Expectations:

Students will:

- become more knowledgeable and better acquainted with the location, physical features, climate, bodies of water, boundaries, agriculture, mineral resources, industries, cities, symbols, and flags of the Prairie Provinces.
- develop reading and research skills to locate answers requested.
- identify and label maps of Manitoba, Saskatchewan, and Alberta.

A. Reproduce the information sheet called **"The Prairie Provinces"** found on **page 99** for your students to read independently or display the page on a white board for large group reading and discussion.

Brainstorm on three single charts labelled Manitoba, Saskatchewan, and Alberta various facts the students know about these three provinces. List questions on another chart that they want answered about the prairie provinces.

Have the students read the information in each paragraph. Then have students locate the sentence in which the answer appears and have one of them underline it and read it aloud.

Paragraph #1:

What are the names of the three prairie provinces? (*Manitoba, Saskatchewan, Alberta*) What are the three physical features in Manitoba? (*Hudson Bay Lowlands, The Canadian Shield, the first level of the Interior Plain or Plateau*) What is the physical feature found in Saskatchewan? (*the second level of the Interior Plain or Plateau*) What physical feature is found in Alberta? (*the third level of the Interior Plain or Plateau*) If you travelled from east to west in the Prairie Provinces, what happens to the land? (*It gets progressively higher.*)

Paragraph #2:

What is a "prairie?" (*a large grassy land with no trees*) Where is the prairie region located in the three Prairie Provinces? (*stretches from the foothills of the Rocky Mountains in the west to the Red River in the east*) Locate this area on a wall map. What do you find in the northern area of each province? (*evergreen forests*)

Paragraph #3:

Which prairie province has the largest population? (*Alberta*) Can you think of reasons why it has the most people living in it? (*Answers will vary.*) Which prairie province has the lowest population? (*Saskatchewan*) Can you think of reasons why it has the lowest population? (*Answers will vary.*) Which prairie province has the second highest population? (*Manitoba*) In what part of the Prairie Provinces do most of the people live? (*southern part*) Tell why. (*great for wheat farming as the land is flat and fertile*) Where is cattle ranching done? (*hilly parts of the Prairie Provinces, where it is dry*)

Paragraph #4:

What else is found in the Prairie Provinces? (*minerals, gas, oil, nickel, copper, potash*)

Prairie Provinces

Paragraph #5:

What is the name of the capital city of Manitoba? (*Winnipeg*) What is the capital city of Saskatchewan? (*Regina*) What is the capital city of Alberta? (*Edmonton*) What are the names of some of the other important cities in the Prairie Provinces? (*Calgary, Saskatoon, Banff, Jasper, Prince Albert*)

Paragraph #6 and #7:

What is the climate like in the prairie region? (*drier than in other regions*) Why is the climate in the Prairie Region drier? (*moist winds from the Pacific Ocean are blocked by the Rocky Mountains causing the air to be drier*) What are winters like on the prairies? (*long, windy, very cold, sunny and bright*) How much rain falls in the summer? (*amount varies from year to year; falls in showers*) How do summers in the Prairies vary? (*sometimes summers are very dry or they are very wet; summers are usually warm and sunny*) What do the Prairie Provinces have the most of in Canada? (*three quarters of Canada's cropland*)

B. Worksheets found on pages 100 to 111 are to be used as research and mapping activities and reproduced for groups of students. Each group will research using the Internet, reference books, atlases, and wall maps to find the missing information to complete each worksheet. With the worksheets called "Manitoba's Cities," "Saskatchewan's Cities" and "Alberta's Cities" are maps for each province to be completed as well. All answers are to be recorded on the sheets. When all the groups are finished and they have checked their answers with the Answer Key, they could present what they have learned about the Prairie Provinces.

Answer Key for Worksheet #1: Location and Surface page 100

Location: a) **Manitoba** - North Border: Nunavut, Hudson Bay; West Border: Saskatchewan; East Border: Ontario; South Border: The United States b) **Saskatchewan** - North Border: Nunavut; West Border: Alberta; East Border: Manitoba; South Border: The United States c) **Alberta** - North Border: Northwest Territories; West Border: British Columbia; East Border: Saskatchewan; South Border: The United States

Surface:

1. A slough is a soft, deep, muddy place or mud hole; marshy area. 2. a) Manitoba: Hudson Bay Lowlands, the Canadian Shield, Interior Plains or Plateau. b) Saskatchewan: Interior Plains or Plateau c) Alberta: Interior Plains or Plateau 3. A prairie is flat land covered with long grasses and very few trees. 4. Trees are rare on the prairies because it is difficult for them to compete with the grasses and wildflowers. They cannot adapt to the harsh prairie climate. 5. The land becomes very dry because there is no rainfall. There is a lack of rain for an extended period of time. 6. The soil is rich and fertile. 7. The main causes are drought, flooding, and an early frost.

Answer Key for Worksheet #2: Climate page 101

Climate: 1. Manitoba: winter; •southeastern; north; • sunlight; sunniest; • short; frost; permafrost; • central; snow; rain; overflow; flood; • the Red River 2. **Saskatchewan:** • extreme; long; cold; short; hot; • pleasant; wind; • continental; rainfall; snowfall; sunshine; • drought; colder
3. **Alberta:** • changeable; snow; •July; August; hottest; Indian Summer; warm; cold; • October; March; blizzards; wind chill; winds; visability; • January; quickly; wind direction; west; arch; clouds; chinook; temperature

Prairie Provinces

Answer Key for Worksheet #3: Agriculture page 102.
Agriculture: Manitoba: 1. • Farming; wheat; • canola; barley; flaxseed; oats; rye; • flax; • livestock; • 300 hectares; • grain; elevators; • centre; • chemicals; fertilizers; farm machinery
2. **Saskatchewan:** • third; • wheat; oats; canola; sunflowers; lentils; canary seed; cattle; hogs; chickens; turkeys; eggs; milk; honey; vegetables; • wheat; • 400; • fewer; • prices; government
3. **Alberta:** • wheat; canola; cattle; dairy products; vegetables; • Japan; United States; • changing; larger; fewer; land; machinery; crops
4. Soil is rich and fertile. They receive a good amount of rainfall. They have a slightly longer growing season. The summer climate is quite warm

Answer Key for Worksheets #4 and #5: Industries pages 103 to 104.
Industries:
1. **Manitoba:** a) processed foods; transportation equipment; printing; publishing; clothing; textiles; machinery; b) Nickel; Copper; Flin Flon; zinc; gold; lead; cobalt; tantalum; tellurium; c) rivers; lakes; hydro-electric; Winnipeg; Saskatchewan; Nelson; d) Petroleum; natural gas; e) The Pas; Pine Falls; f) Pinawa
2. **Saskatchewan:** a) minerals; petroleum; • Potash; fertilizer; • uranium; exporter; • gold; zinc; salt; clay; b) oil; gas; • Regina; Lloydminister; • heavy oil; • recover; refine; c) Lignite; stations; d) Manufacturing; steel; fertilizer; street sweepers; ambulances; steel-makers; Regina; e) logging; pulp; paper; small; heavily forested
3. **Alberta:** a) "Energy Province;" oil; crude; heavy; sands; sweet; sour; furnaces; exported; sold; b) food; beverage; chemicals; electronics; machinery; c) forestry; commercialized; logging roads; over use; damage; pulp; paper; Athabasca; Peace; herbicides; ecosystem; humans; wildlife; aquatic; d) United States; Pacific Rim; Grand Prairie; Hinton; Slave Lake; High Level; White Court; High Prairie; Fox Creek; Athabasca; e) United States; England; China; Japan; Korea; oil; gas; food; machinery; farm; building; motor vehicles; retail; Mall; f) Tourism; scenery; Rocky Mountains; Banff; Jasper

Answer Key for Worksheet #6: Manitoba's Cities and Mapping Skills pages 105 to106
1. a) **Map of Manitoba: Cities and Towns:** 1. Lynn Lake 2. Flin Flon 3. The Pas 4 Brandon
5. Portage La Prairie 6. Winnipeg 7. Selkirk 8. Churchill
Lakes: 1. Lake Winnipeg 2. Lake Winnipegosis 3. Lake Manitoba **Rivers:** 1. Assiniboine River
2. Souris River 3. Red River 4. Winnipeg River 5. Hayes River 6. Nelson River 7. Churchill River
2. a) Red River b) Assiniboine River c) Assiniboine d) Assiniboine e) Ochre River
3. a) capital city of Manitoba; largest city b) Manitoba's second largest city c) important trading fort during the fur trading era d) Copper is mined here. e) Pulp and paper centre; forestry
f) salt water port; place to watch polar bears play in the fall g) has one of Canada's longest suspension footbridges

Answer Key for Worksheet #7: Saskatchewan's Cities and Mapping Skills pages 107 to 108
1. a) **Map of Saskatchewan: Cities and Towns:** 1. Uranium City 2. Lloydminister 3. North Battlefield 4. Saskatoon 5. Swift Current 6. Moose Jaw 7. Regina 8. Weyburn 9. Estevan
10. Prince Albert 11. Yorkton

b) **Lakes:** 1. Lake Athabasca 2. Cree Lake 3. Lac La Ronge 4. Reindeer Lake 5. Wollaston Lake

c) **Rivers:** 1. Cree River 2. North Saskatchewan River 3. South Saskatchewan River
4. Qu'Appelle River 5. Souris River

2. a) North Saskatchewan River b) South Saskatchewan River c) North Saskatchewan River
d) Souris River e) Qu'Appelle River

3. a) the largest city in Saskatchewan b) the home of W.O. Mitchell, a famous Canadian author who wrote the book "Who Has Seen the Wind?" c) one of Saskatchewan's major oil and coal producing cities d) capital city of Saskatchewan; second largest city in the province; R.C.M.P school is here e) Prince Albert National Park; contains the cabin and gravesite of Grey Owl (a park ranger) f) has the world's largest tomahawk

Answer Key for Worksheet #8: Alberta's Cities and Mapping Skills pages 109 to 111
1. a) **Map of Alberta: Cities and Towns:** 1. Grand Prairie 2. Jasper 3. Banff 4. Calgary
5. Drumheller 6. Medicine Hat 7. Lethbridge 8. Red Deer 9. Wetaskiwun 10. Camrose
11. Lloydminister 12. Edmonton

b) **Lakes:** 1. Bistcho Lake 2. Lake Athabasca 3. Lake Claire 4. Utikuma Lake 5. Lesser Slave Lake **Rivers:** 1. Peace River 2. Athabasca River 3. North Saskatchewan River 4. Red Deer River 5. Bow River 6. South Saskatchewan River

2. a) North Saskatchewan River b) Bow River c) South Saskatchewan River d) South Saskatchewan River e) Red Deer River f) Red Deer River g) Athabasca River

3.a) holds the Calgary Stampede; largest city in Alberta; has Calgary Olympic Park b) a famous national park; beautiful mountain scenery; tourist attraction; Lake Louise c) Red Deer River Badlands; hoo doos; Museum of Palaeontology d) capital city of Alberta e) large oil field
f) gigantic, aluminum Ukrainian Easter Egg

Answer Key for Worksheet #9: Lakes and Rivers and Tourist Attractions page 110
a) **Lakes and Rivers:** 1. Lake Winnipeg 2. Lake Athabaska 3. Lake Manitoba 4. Manitoba
5. Dauphin River; Red River 6. Nelson River; Churchill River; Hayes River 7. South Saskatchewan River

b) **Tourist Attractions:** 1. Drumheller, Alberta 2. CFB Moose Jaw, Saskatchewan 3. Churchill, Manitoba 4. Calgary, Alberta 5. Alberta 6. Banff or Jasper, Alberta 7. Regina, Saskatchewan
8. Drumheller, Alberta 9. Vegreville, Alberta 10. Jasper, Alberta 11. Churchill, Manitoba
12. Drumheller, Alberta 13. Saskatchewan 14. Saskatchewan

Prairie Provinces

Information Sheet

Manitoba's Flag

Manitoba's Flower: Prairie Crocus

Saskatchewan's Flag

Saskatchewan's Flower: Prairie Lily

Alberta's Flag

Alberta's Flower: Wild Rose

The provinces of Manitoba, Saskatchewan, and Alberta make up the prairie region. Manitoba has three main physical features. They are the Hudson Bay Lowlands, The Canadian Shield and the first level of the Interior Plain or Plateau. Saskatchewan consists of the second level of the Interior Plain or Plateau. Alberta is entirely made up of the third level of the Interior Plain or Plateau. Each level of the Interior Plain becomes progressively higher as you proceed from east to west.

Located in the southern part of each province is a large triangular-shaped land area called a "prairie." A prairie is a large grassland with very few trees. Canada's prairie region stretches from the foothills of the Rocky Mountains in the west to the Red River in the east. The northern area of each province is covered with evergreen forests.

The three Prairie Provinces occupy 1 963 470 square kilometres of Canada's land area. The total population in the prairie region is 5 886 906 (2011 census). Most of the people live in the southern part of each province or prairie area. Large wheat farms are found here, as the land is very fertile and flat. Cattle ranching is found on the drier hilly parts of the prairie region.

Winnipeg is the capital city of Manitoba and the province has a population of 1 208 268 (2011 census). Regina is the capital city of Saskatchewan and the province's population is 1 033 381 (2011 census). The capital city of Alberta is Edmonton and the province has a population of 3 645 257 (2011 census). The provincial government for each province is found in each capital city.

The Prairie Provinces are also rich in minerals. Oil and gas wells are seen throughout this region. Nickel and copper mines are found in the north. Potash is also mined and used to make fertilizer.

The prairie region experiences a much drier climate than other regions of Canada. The Rocky Mountains block the moist winds from the Pacific Ocean, causing the air to be dry. Winters are long, windy, and very cold, but days are often sunny and very bright. During the summer, rain falls as showers and the amount varies from year to year. Some years it can be too dry and other years it may be too wet. Summers are usually warm and sunny.

The prairie region is very rich in agricultural and mineral resources. Three quarters of Canada's total cropland is found in the Prairie Provinces.

SSJ192 ISBN 9781771586900

Prairie Provinces

Worksheet #1: Location and Surface

Location:

1. Give the boundaries of:
   a) **Manitoba:**
   North Border - _____
   West Border - _____
   East Border - _____
   South Border - _____
   b) **Saskatchewan:**
   North Border - _____
   West Border - _____
   East Border _____
   South Border - _____
   c) **Alberta:**
   North Border - _____
   West Border - _____
   East Border - _____
   South Border - _____

Surface:

1. What is a slough? _____
   _____

2. The Prairie Provinces are each divided into three main physical regions.
   a) **Manitoba** contains the _____, _____ and the
   first level of the _____ or _____.
   b) **Saskatchewan** consists of the second level of the _____ or
   _____.
   c) **Alberta** consists of the third level of the _____ or
   _____.

3. What does a prairie look like? _____
   _____

4. Why are there few trees on the prairies? _____
   _____
   _____

5. What is a drought? _____
   _____

6. Why are prairie farmers successful at growing grain in these provinces?
   _____
   _____

7. What are the chief causes of crop failure in the Prairie Provinces?
   _____
   _____

Prairie Provinces

Worksheet #2: Climate

1. **Manitoba's** climate can vary greatly. In the _____, the average temperature may be -19.3°C in January, while in the summer in July it can be as hot as 19.6°C.

• The _____ part of the province receives the most precipitation and the _____ receives the least.

• Manitoba enjoys plenty of _____ all year long. It is one of North America's _____ spots.

• In the northern part of the province, the summers are so _____ that _____ stays in the ground year-round. This is called _____.

• In _____ Manitoba, the land is quite flat and a fast _____ melt or too much spring _____ causes the rivers and streams to _____ their banks and _____ the countryside.

• What is the name of the river in Manitoba that did overflow its banks in 1950?

_____

2. **Saskatchewan's** climate is quite _____. It suffers from _____, bitterly _____ winters and extremely _____ _____ summers.

• Spring and fall are quite _____. There is a constant _____ during all the seasons.

• Saskatchewan's climate is known as _____ with low _____ and _____ on the plains and lots of _____.

• The plains area often suffers from _____. In northern Saskatchewan, winters are much _____, with temperatures around -40°C.

3. **Alberta** has a very _____ climate. It has been known that near the mountains the weather can change suddenly. In early May, the _____ melts in the mountains, except on the higher peaks, where it stays all summer long.

• Alberta's warmest months are _____ and _____. July is usually the _____ month. Autumn is beautiful in Alberta, as _____ _____ is experienced after the first frosts. The days are _____, but the nights are _____.

• Snow in Alberta lasts for five or six months and comes in _____ and stays until _____. In the winter, the prairies receive _____ that are dangerous with a high _____ factor, high _____, and poor _____.

• The coldest month is _____. Temperatures in the winter can rise or fall _____ depending on the _____ _____. Winds from the _____ and an _____ of _____ signal the arrival of a _____. A chinook is a warm, dry wind that raises the _____ as much as 25 degrees and melts all the snow on the ground quickly.

Prairie Provinces

Worksheet # 3: Agriculture

Manitoba

1. • _____ is Manitoba's most important industry . _____ is the main crop grown.
   • Other crops such as _____, _____, _____, _____, and _____ are grown.
   • Manitoba is one of the world's major producers of _____.
   • _____ production is the second largest farming industry.
   • The average size of a farm in Manitoba is _____ _____.
   • Manitoba's grain is held in 300 or more _____ _____ throughout the province.
   • It is a _____ for marketing and transporting grain to other places.
   • Agricultural _____, _____ and _____ _____ are manufactured in the province.

Saskatchewan

2. • Saskatchewan is the _____ largest agricultural producer in Canada.
   • It produces immense crops of _____, _____, _____, _____, _____, and _____. It also produces large quantities of _____, _____, _____, _____, _____, _____, _____, and _____.
   • Of all the products produced in Saskatchewan, _____ is still the most important.
   • An average farm in Saskatchewan is _____ hectares.
   • There are now _____ farms as smaller farms have been bought to form larger ones.
   • Unfortunately, there are years when wheat _____ are low and the _____ has to help the farmers with their expenses.

Alberta

3. • Alberta's major agricultural crops produced are _____, _____, and _____. Poultry, _____, and _____ are also produced.
   • Many products are exported to _____ and the _____.
   • Farms in Alberta are _____. They are getting _____ but _____. Larger farms can use the _____ and expensive _____ more economically. New _____ have been introduced due to low prices for wheat, barley, and rye.

4. Why are all the Prairie Provinces suited for farming? Think of four good reasons.

   _____
   _____
   _____
   _____

Prairie Provinces

Worksheet #4: Industries

Manitoba

1.a) Manitoba's leading manufactured products are: _____

_____

_____

_____

b) _____ is the main mineral mined for in Manitoba's mines. _____ is
the second most important metal. _____ is where most of the province's
copper is produced. Other important metals are _____, _____,
_____, _____, _____, and _____.

c) Manitoba has plenty of _____ and _____ and is able to produce its
own _____ - _____ power. Power is produced on the
_____, _____, and _____ Rivers.

d) _____ and _____ are produced near Viren.

e) Pulp and paper are produced at _____ and _____.

f) One of Canada's nuclear research centres is located at _____ on the Winnipeg
River.

Saskatchewan

2.a) Saskatchewan's ground is also very rich with _____ and _____.
_____ is exported all over the world to make _____.
Saskatchewan has three mines that produce _____, and it is the world's largest
_____.

The province also produces _____, copper, _____,
_____, sand, gravel, and _____.

b) Saskatchewan is also a major producer of _____ and _____.
_____ and _____ have refineries that process heavy oil.
The province has the world's largest reserve of _____ _____ which is a thick,
sludgy mixture of oil and sand. It is very expensive to _____ and _____.

c) _____ coal, which burns quickly and gives off less heat, is mined in
Saskatchewan. It is used at power- generating _____ throughout the province.

d) _____ has steadily increased in the province. Many manufacturers are small
and produce products such as _____, _____, _____,
_____, diapers, and enamel pins. One of the largest _____ is
located in _____. Other industries include food-processing, printing, machinery,
metal products, wood, and electronic machines.

e) There is some _____ and _____ and _____ mills are found in the province.
This type of industry is relatively _____, even though a large part of Northern
Saskatchewan is _____ _____.

Prairie Provinces

Worksheet # 5: Industries
Alberta

3.a) Alberta is known as the _____ _____ due to its abundant _____ resources. Alberta has three types of oil resources. They are _____ oil, _____ oil, and oil _____. There are two kinds of natural gas, which are _____ gas and _____ gas. Sweet gas is the type burned in household _____. The refined gas is _____ to California and other States and _____ to other parts of Canada.

b) The largest manufacturing business is the _____ and _____ industries. Other industries are clothing, food products, furniture, forest products, _____, _____, telecommunications, and _____.

c) Alberta's _____ industry is rapidly growing, and many people are concerned about its effects. The people do not want the forests to become _____. They fear the _____ _____ will allow the public to _____ _____ and _____ the natural forest. There are concerns that _____ and _____ mills will pollute or harm the _____ and _____ Rivers. People are concerned about the effect that _____ will have on the forest's _____, _____, _____, and _____ life.

d) Lumber, pulp, wood products, poles, and other wood products are exported to the _____ and the _____ countries. Lumbering areas are found near centres such as _____, _____, _____, _____, _____, _____, _____, and _____.

e) Alberta trades with countries such as the _____, _____, _____, _____, and _____. The items traded are _____, _____, _____ products, _____, _____ products, _____ materials , and _____. Most of the trade workers are imployed in the _____ industry. Edmonton's West Edmonton _____ is internationally known.

f) _____ is an important industry in Alberta. Its spectacular _____ is in the _____. _____ and _____ are national parks that attract millions of tourists from all over the world.

SSJ192 ISBN 9781771586900

Prairie Provinces

Worksheet #6: Manitoba's Cities and Mapping Skills

1. a) On the map of Manitoba, locate and name the following cities. Locate and name the capital city. It has a star in a circle on the map. Each city is represented by a dot and a line. Print the names neatly on the lines.

Brandon	**Portage La Prairie**	**Flin Flon**	**Winnipeg**
The Pas	**Churchill**	**Selkirk**	**Lynn Lake**

b) On the map of Manitoba, locate and label the following rivers and lakes. Each lake and river is represented by a numeral inside a circle. Print the names neatly on the lines.

Lake Winnipeg	**Lake Manitoba**	**Lake Winnipegosis**	**Winnipeg River**
Assiniboine River	**Churchill River**	**Nelson River**	**Hayes River**
Red River	**Souris River**		

2. The cities below are located on rivers. Locate a map and then locate the river that it is on.

   a) Winnipeg is on the _____.

   b) Portage la Prairie is found on the _____.

   c) Brandon is located on the _____.

   d) Grand Falls is found on the _____.

   e) Dauphin is found on the _____.

3. Tell why each of the following cities is important.

   a) Winnipeg: _____

   _____

   b) Brandon: _____

   _____

   c) Portage La Prairie: _____

   _____

   d) Flin Flon: _____

   _____

   e) The Pas: _____

   _____

   f) Churchill: _____

   _____

   g) Souris: _____

   _____

SSJ192 ISBN 9781771586900

Map of Manitoba

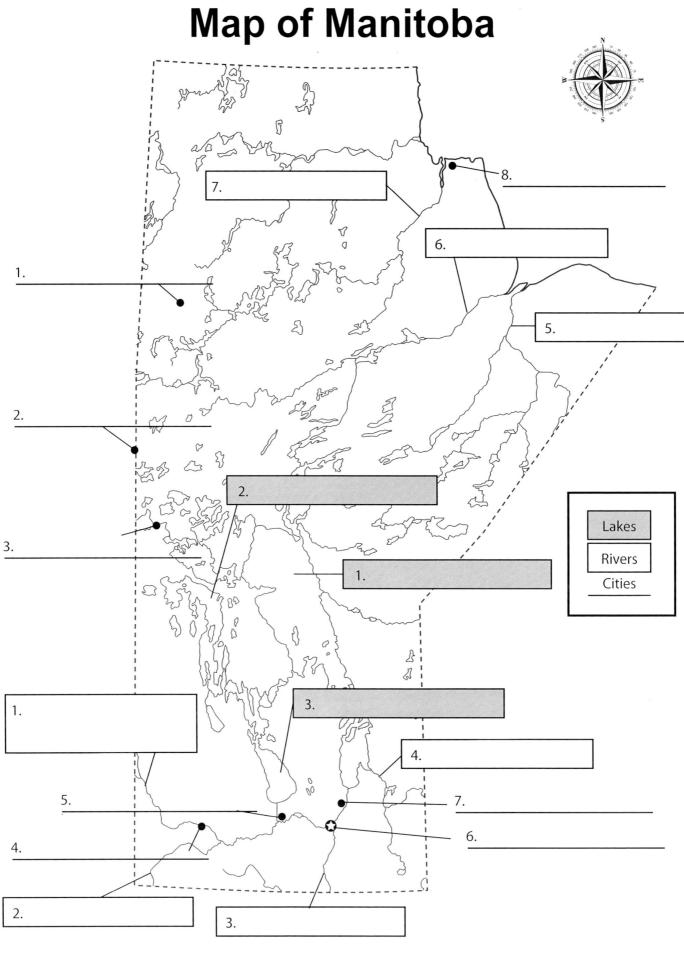

Legend:
- Lakes
- Rivers
- Cities

SSJ192 ISBN 9781771586900

Prairie Provinces

Worksheet #7: Saskatchewan's Cities and Mapping Skills

1. a) On the map of Saskatchewan, locate the following cities. The cities are marked with a dot and a line. The capital city is marked with a circled star. Print each name neatly on the line provided.

Regina	**Saskatoon**	**North Battleford**	**Weyburn**	**Swift Current**
Yorkton	**Uranium City**	**Moose Jaw**	**Estevan**	**Lloydminister**
Prince Albert				

   b) Find and label the following lakes and rivers. Each lake is marked with a line coming from a shaded box. Print its name in the shaded box. Each river has a line pointing from a white box. Print the name in its box.

Lake Athabasca	**Wollaston Lake**	**Reindeer Lake**
Lac La Ronge	**Qu'Appelle River**	**South Saskatchewan River**
Cree River	**Souris River**	**North Saskatchewan River**

   c) Colour all the other lakes and rivers blue

2. The cities below are located on rivers. Locate the city on a map and then locate the river that it is on.

   a) North Battleford is on the _____ .

   b) Saskatoon is on the _____ .

   c) Prince Albert is on the _____ .

   d) Weyburn is on the _____ .

   e) Fort Qu'Appelle is on the _____ .

3. Tell why each of the following cities is important.

   a) Saskatoon: _____

   _____

   b) Weyburn: _____

   _____

   c) Estevan: _____

   _____

   d) Regina: _____

   _____

   e) Prince Albert: _____

   _____

   f) Batouche: _____

   _____

Map of Saskatchewan

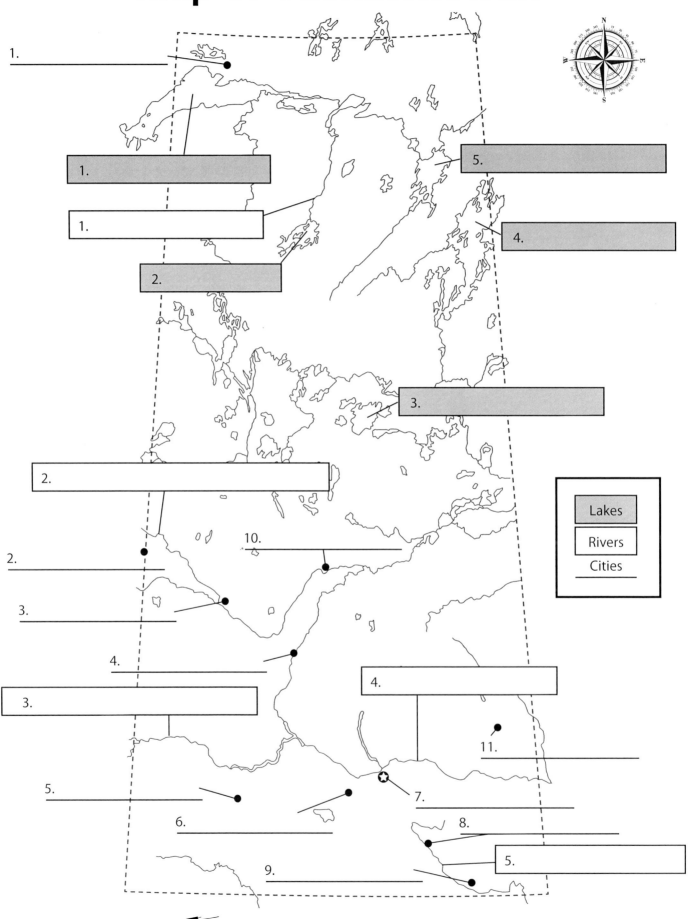

1. _____

1. [_____]

1. [_____]

2. [_____]

5. [_____]

4. [_____]

3. [_____]

2. [_____]

10. _____

2. _____

3. _____

4. _____

3. [_____]

4. [_____]

11. _____

5. _____

6. _____

7. _____

8. _____

5. [_____]

9. _____

Lakes

Rivers

Cities

SSJ192 ISBN 9781771586900

Prairie Provinces

Worksheet #8: Alberta's Cities and Mapping Skills

1. a) On the accompanying map, locate the following cities. The cities are marked with a dot. Print each name neatly on the line provided. The capital city is marked with a circled star.

Edmonton	Lethbridge	Red Deer	Calgary
Medicine Hat	Camrose	Grande Prairie	Wetaskiwin
Drumheller	Lloydminister	Banff	Jasper

   b) Name the following lakes and rivers. Each lake is marked with a line coming from a shaded box. Print its name in the shaded box. Each river has a line pointing from a white box. Print the name in its box.

Lake Athabaska	Lake Claire	Lesser Slave Lake	Utikuma Lake
Bistcho Lake	Bow River	South Saskatchewan River	Athabasca River
Red Deer River	Peace River	North Saskatchewan River	

   c) Colour all the other lakes and rivers blue.

2. The cities below are located on rivers. Locate the city on a map and then locate the river it is on.

   a) Edmonton is located on the _____.

   b) Calgary is found on the _____.

   c) Lethbridge is on the _____.

   d) Medicine Hat is located on the _____.

   e) Red Deer is found on the _____.

   f) Drumheller is on the _____.

   g) Fort McMurray is on the _____.

3. Tell why each of the following cities in Alberta are important.

   a) Calgary: _____

   _____

   b) Banff: _____

   _____

   c) Drumheller: _____

   _____

   d) Edmonton: _____

   _____

   e) Leduc: _____

   _____

   f) Vegreville: _____

   _____

Map of Alberta

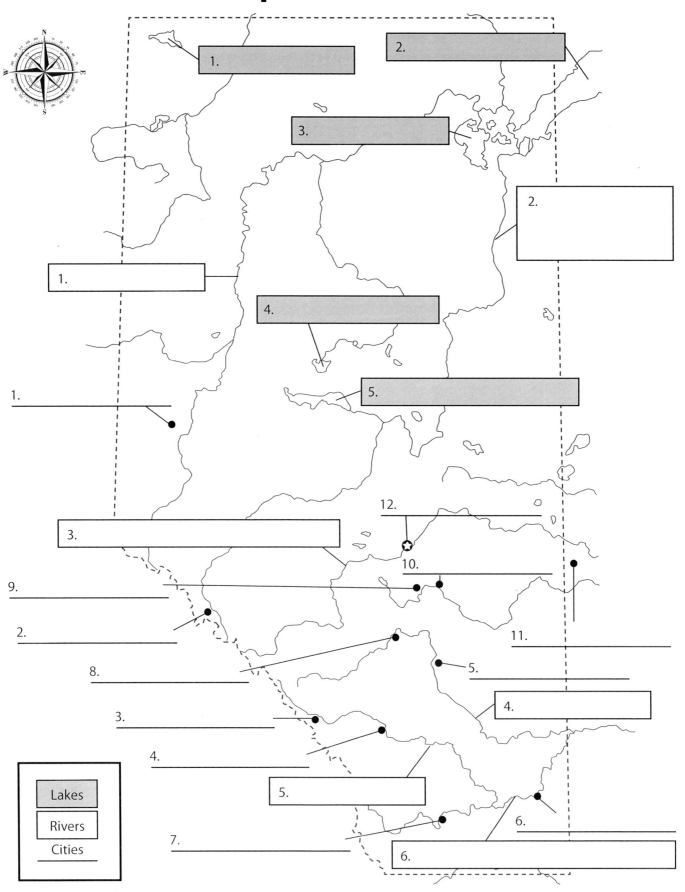

Lakes

Rivers

Cities

SSJ138 ISBN 9781770789487

Prairie Provinces

Worksheet #9: Lakes and Rivers and Tourist Attractions

Lakes and Rivers:

Using your mapping skills, locate on a map the correct place and underline its name in each sentence or for each question.

1. The largest lake in the Prairie Provinces is (Lake Athabasca, Cree Lake, Lake Winnipeg, Cedar Lake, Frobisher Lake, Lake Manitoba, Island Lake)

2. The most northerly lake is (God's Lake, Reindeer Lake, Southern Indian Lake, Lake Athabasca, Lac La Ronge, Lake Winnipegosis, Lake Dauphin).

3. The most southerly lake is (Churchill Lake, Lesser Slave Lake, Lake Louise, Lake Manitoba, Moose Lake, Wollaston Lake).

4. Most lakes are located in (Manitoba, Saskatchewan, Alberta).

5. Underline the two rivers that flow into Lake Winnipeg. (Peace River, Athabasca River, Hayes River, Dauphin River, Red River).

6. Which three rivers flow into Hudson Bay? (Nelson River, Saskatchewan River, Athabasca River, Churchill River, Qu'Appelle River, Hayes River, Winnipeg River, Red River)

7. Which river flows through all three Prairie Provinces? (North Saskatchewan River, Peace River, Hayes River, South Saskatchewan River, Red River, Nelson River)

Tourist Attractions:

Where in the Prairie Provinces would you find the following tourist attractions? Write the name of the city or town and its province on the line at the end of the attraction.

1. the Red Deer Badlands: _____

2. the Snowbirds, Canada's famous flying team: _____

3. real polar bears: _____

4. a famous western Stampede: _____

5. cattle ranches: _____

6. a famous National Park: _____

7. a school for Royal Canadian Mounted Police: _____

8. rock formations called Hoodoos: _____

9. a gigantic Ukrainian Easter Egg: _____

10. glaciers and icefields: _____

11. a salt water harbour: _____

12. a dinosaur museum: _____

13. oil wells in fields pumping oil: _____

14. lots of grain elevators: _____

British Columbia

Lesson Plan #16: British Columbia

Expectations:

Students will:

• become more knowledgeable and better acquainted with the location, physical features, climate, bodies of water, boundaries, agriculture, mineral resources, industries, cities, symbols, and flag of the province of British Columbia.
• develop reading and research skills to locate answers requested.
• identify and label maps of British Columbia.

A. Reproduce the information sheets called "British Columbia" found on pages 115 to 116 for your students to read independently or display them on a white board for large group reading and discussion.

Brainstorm for information that the students know about British Columbia. The points could be recorded on a chart. Questions that students have about this province could be recorded and answered on another chart.

Have your students read the information in each paragraph(s). Then have them locate answers to the following questions.

Information Sheet #1 British Columbia page 115

Paragraph #1: What is the name of Canada's most western province? (*British Columbia*) What else is it called? (*most western province; Pacific Province*) Why is it called the Pacific Province? (*coastline is on the Pacific Ocean*) What is the name of the main physical region in British Columbia? (*North American Cordillera*) How far does this region stretch? (*from the tip of Alaska, along the coast of North America to the southern part of Central America*) Show your students this region on a wall map.

Paragraph #2: What are the six main land regions in British Columbia? (*Insular Mountains; Lower Fraser Valley; Coast Mountains; Interior Plateau; Eastern Mountains [Rocky Mountains] Transmontane Plains*)

Paragraphs #3 to #7: Where are the Insular Mountains found? (*mostly under the ocean; islands along the coast; Vancouver Island; Queen Charlotte Islands*) Which region is found in the southwestern corner of British Columbia's mainland? (*Lower Fraser Valley*) Why is this area a good farming area? (*soils are fertile; climate is mild*) What region extends north westward from the Lower Fraser Valley into the Yukon Territory? (*Coast Mountains*) What do they give British Columbia? (*a high, indented coastline*) What region lies east of the Coast Mountains? (*the Interior Plain*) Why is this an important area? (*important valleys for farming, fruit growing, and cattle grazing*) What is found on the northern part of the plateau? (*forests*) In which region do you find the Rocky Mountains? (*Eastern Mountains*) How far do the Rocky Mountains extend? (*runs north and south from Montana [U.S.] to the Yukon Territory*) What are names of the rivers that flow through the Rocky Mountain Trench? (*Kootenay; Columbia; Fraser; Parsnip; Finlay*) Where are the Transmontane Plains located? (*northeastern corner of the province*) What is the land like in this region? (*flat and hilly*) What famous district is found in this region? (*Peace River District*)

British Columbia

Paragraph #8: Describe British Columbia's coastline. (*narrow inlets, Inside Passageway – narrow waterway*) What does British Columbia have in large quantities? (*lakes and rivers*) Where do many lakes drain? (*into the Pacific Ocean*)

Paragraph #9: What is the population of British Columbia? (*4 400 057; 2011 census*) Where do most of the people live in British Columbia? (*Vancouver-Victoria Region; southwestern corner of British Columbia*) Why is Vancouver an important city? (*largest and busiest port in Canada*) What is the name of the capital city? (*Victoria*) Where is it located? (*eastern tip of Vancouver Island*) How do goods and people travel between Vancouver Island and the mainland? (*ferries*)

Information Sheet #2: British Columbia page 116
Paragraph #1: Describe British Columbia's climate. (*mild, wet all year long along the coast; winter is rainy; temperatures above freezing; summers are warm, less rain; interior valleys are warm; winters are cold and the ground is snow-covered; skies are clear and blue; northern interior areas are cold; high mountains are snow-capped all year*)

Paragraph #2: What are the two main natural resources in British Columbia? (*forests, minerals*) What are two important industries in British Columbia? (*logging, mining*) What minerals are mined in British Columbia? (*copper, coal, zinc, lead*) What are the main industries in British Columbia? (*food and beverage processing; wood products; paper products*) What industry in British Columbia is the largest in Canada? (*fishing*) What type of fish are mainly caught? (*salmon*) What are the Fraser and Okanagan Valleys famous for? (*farming*) What other industry is important to British Columbia? (*tourism*) Why do tourists like to visit British Columbia? (*to view the beautiful scenery and to visit tourist attractions*)

Answers Key for Worksheet #1: Location and Surface page 117

Location: 1. most westerly province 2. Alberta 3. the Northwest Territories and the Yukon 4. the United States 5. its west coast 6. highly indented 7. part of the state of Alaska

Surface: 1. The Cordilleran Region 2. Pacific Ocean 3. indented 4. Rocky Mountains 5. Cassair Mountains, Columbia Mountains, Purcell Mountains, Cariboo Mountains, Coast Mountains, Selkirk Mountains, Cascade Mountains, Omineca Mountains 6. Vancouver Island; Queen Charlotte Islands 7. Kicking Horse Pass, Crowsnest Pass, Yellowhead Pass 8. It lies between the Coast Mountains and the Rocky Mountains

Answers Key for Worksheet #2: Climate and Industries page 118

Climate: varied, mountains, lake, different, Vancouver Island, lush, green, forested, Gulf islands, rainshadow, drier, warmer; interior, hotter, drier, summer, colder, winter, mild, warm, cool, Moist, autumn, winter, mountains, rain, dry; long, cold, hot

Industries:
Forestry: Thousands, exports; harvested, lumber, pulp, paper, shingles, shakes; loggers, truck-drivers, planters; important, conserved, replaced; conflicts; logging; clear-cutting, removal; land claims; Forest, workers, resort, operators; mill owners; Environmentalists; Commission; forest industry, environment

British Columbia

Mining: mountains; Gold, coal, sulphur, copper, zinc; miners, prospectors; Cassiar, asbestos; Kitimat; sulphur; Coal, southern, Okanagan, important; dependable, disappear, community, main

Energy: energy, resources; five, Pacific Rim; Oil, gas, Westcoast Energy Pipeline; Electricity, Peace, Fraser, Skeena, Columbia, dams; hydro-electric

Tourism: scenery, mild; Vancouver, Victoria; mountains, winter; golfers, cyclists; wildlife

Fishing: business; thousands; forty, fish, marine; fish-processing, fish, salmon, shellfish; fleets; operators, biologists, workers, farmers; Prince Rupert, Steveston; pinks, sockeye, coho, chum, chinook; highly, fresh, frozen, canned; half; exports; Herring, eggs, roe; spring; female, Japan; bodies, animal food, fertilizer; shrinking; commercial, sport, Aboriginal

Answer Key for Worksheet #3: British Columbia's Cities page 121
1. Vancouver, largest, busiest; natural, harbour, freezes; all year; Japan, Asian; Canada's Gateway to the Pacific; beautiful; Pacific Ocean; Coast Mountains; climate; mountains; warm winds; climate, scenery; Chinese; Indian; Japanese; Pacific Rim 2. Victoria: capital; city; southern; Vancouver; Island; Canada's City of Flowers; mild; year-round; Butchart; Gardens; famous; old; historic; Empress; Totem, poles

Mapping Activity: British Columbia's Cities page122
1. Prince Rupert 2. Powell River 3. Vancouver 4. Port Alberni 5. Nanaimo 6. Victoria 7. Duncan 8. New Westminister 9. Penticton 10. Kelowna 11. Kamloops 12. Prince George 13. Dawson Creek 14. Kitimat

Answer Key for Worksheet #4: British Columbia's Waterways page 124
a) True b) False c) False d) True e) True f) False g) True h) True i) False j) False

Mapping Skills: British Columbia's Waterways page 125
1. Pacific Ocean 2. Queen Charlotte Islands 3. Queen Charlotte Strait 4. Juan de Fuca Strait 5. Strait of Georgia 6. Vancouver Island 7. Hecate Strait 8. Laird River 9. Stikine River 10. Nass River 11. Skeena River 12. Babine Lake 13. Williston Lake 14. Fraser River 15. Chilcotin River 16. Quesnel Lake 17. Thompson River 18. Shuswap Lake 19. Okanagan Lake 20. Okanagan River 21. Kootney Lake 22. Columbia River

British Columbia

Information Sheet

Canada's most western province, or "Pacific Province," is British Columbia. It is the third largest province in land area: 947 800 square kilometres. This province's main physical region is called the North American Cordillera, which stretches along the west coast of North America from the tip of Alaska to the southern part of Central America.

In British Columbia, there are six main land regions. They are the Insular Mountains, the Lower Fraser Valley, the Coast Mountains, the Interior Plateau, the Eastern Mountains (Rocky Mountains), and the Transmontane Plains.

The Insular Mountains are part of a mountain range that lies mostly under the ocean. The higher parts form many of the islands along British Columbia's coast. Vancouver island and the Queen Charlotte Islands are the high parts of the submerged mountain range.

The Lower Fraser Valley is a delta region found in the southwestern corner of the mainland. It is the main farming area of the province. Its soils are fertile and its climate is mild.

The Coast Mountains extend northwest from the Lower Fraser Valley into the Yukon Territory. They give British Columbia a high, indented coastland. The Interior Plain lies east of the Coast Mountains. The Nicola, Okanagan, and Thompson Valleys are important farming, fruit-growing and cattle-grazing areas found on the plain. The northern part of the plateau is heavily forested.

The Eastern Mountains include the Rocky Mountains and other ranges. The Rocky Mountain Trench is a long, narrow valley that runs north and south from Montana (U.S.) to the Yukon Territory. The Kootenay, Columbia, Fraser, Parsnip, and Finlay Rivers flow along the trench.

The Transmontane Plains are flat lands and hilly areas that lie in the northeastern corner of the province. The Peace River District is found on these plains.

British Columbia's coastline is 25 725 kilometres long. Many islands and high mountains are found along the coast. Narrow inlets extend far inland. The narrow waterway between the many islands and coast, called the Inside Passageway, provides a safe waterway for ships to travel. Many lakes and rivers are found throughout British Columbia. Many chief rivers drain into the Pacific Ocean.

More than half of the people in British Columbia live in the Vancouver-Victoria region in the southwestern corner of the province. Its population is 4 400 057 (2011 census). Vancouver is its largest city and Canada's busiest port. Other large cities are Surrey, Burnaby, Richmond, Saanich, and Delta. Victoria is its capital city and is located on the eastern tip of Vancouver Island. Ferries carry goods and passengers between Vancouver Island and the mainland.

British Columbia

The climate in British Columbia is mild and wet all year along the coast. Winter is rainy with temperatures usually above freezing. Summer is warm with less rain. Interior valleys experience a drier climate. The mountains prevent much of the moist Pacific air from blowing inland.

Summers in the interior valleys are warm, while winters are cold and snow covers the ground. Skies are usually clear and blue. Northern areas are also dry, but colder during the winter. On the mountains, it is always cold, and the highest mountains are always snow-capped all year.

Forests and minerals are British Columbia's main natural resources. The forests found along the coast contain evergreen trees that grow very large, such as the Douglas fir and red cedar. The interior valleys are covered in forests as well, but the trees are smaller. Logging and mining are important industries in British Columbia. Minerals such as copper, coal, zinc, and lead are mined. Many wood and paper products are manufactured in British Columbia, and many foods and beverages are processed as well. British Columbia's fishing industry is the largest in Canada. Salmon is the main seafood caught. Farming is mainly done in the southern areas, such as the Fraser Valley and the Okanagan Valley. Tourism plays an important role in British Columbia's economy. People from all over the world come to view its beautiful scenery, ski and snowboard in its mountains, and visit its many tourist attractions.

Buchart Gardens on Vancouver Island

British Columbia

Worksheet #1: Location and Surface

A. Location:

Complete each sentence with the correct ending. Write the ending on the line.

```
. . . . . . . . . . . . . . . . . . . . . . . . . . . . . . . . . . . . . . . . . . . . . . . . . . . . .
                        Sentence Endings

   • Alberta                      • part of the state of Alaska
   • the United States            • the Northwest Territories and the Yukon
   • highly indented              • most westerly province
   • its west coast
. . . . . . . . . . . . . . . . . . . . . . . . . . . . . . . . . . . . . . . . . . . . . . . . . . . . .
```

1. British Columbia is Canada's _____.

2. British Columbia is bounded on the east by _____.

3. It is bounded on the north by _____.

4. It is bounded on the south by _____.

5. The Pacific Ocean washes _____.

6. The western coast of British Columbia is _____.

7. A long part of the western coast is _____.

B. Surface:

Answer each exercise with a sentence.

1. In which physical region of Canada is British Columbia found?

_____

2. What ocean is to the west of British Columbia?

_____

3. Use one word to describe British Columbia's coastline.

_____

4. Which mountain range forms the backbone of British Columbia?

_____

5. Name two other mountain ranges found in British Columbia?

_____

6. What large islands are part of a submerged mountain range in British Columbia?

_____

7. Name three important passes located in the Rocky Mountains.

_____

_____

8. Where is the interior plateau?

_____

_____

British Columbia

Worksheet #2: Climate and Industries

A. Climate:

British Columbia's climate is quite _____. Areas that are separated by _____ or a _____ often experience _____ climates. The west coast of _____ _____ receives over 250 centimetres of rainfall yearly. The island is _____ and _____ and heavily _____. On the opposite side of Vancouver Island lie the _____ _____ in the Strait of Georgia. These islands lie in a _____ and do not receive as much rainfall, so the climate is _____ and _____.

The _____ of the province is _____ and _____ than along the coast in the _____, and _____ in the _____.

_____ winds from the Pacific Ocean _____ British Columbia's coast in the winter and _____ it in the summer. _____ ocean winds bring much rain to the coastal regions, especially in the _____ and _____. If the winds rise over the _____, their moisture turns into _____ and falls on the western slopes. Land east of the mountains remains _____.

Areas to the north have _____, _____ winters; however, their summers are _____ and the growing period is long enough to grow grain and other crops.

B. Industries:
Forestry:

_____ of people work at jobs in the forest industry and the province _____ many forest products. The trees that are _____ are used to make _____, _____ and _____ products, _____, and _____. Workers are _____, biologists, _____, paper mill workers, and tree _____.

The forests are very _____ to all British Columbians. The forests must be _____ or _____ as they are cut. The dwindling supply of trees has caused _____ between forest companies and other groups in the province.

Some groups feel _____ should not be permitted in certain places. Groups are against certain logging methods such as _____, which is the _____ of large areas of forests at one time. These methods may cause damage to the environment. First Nation groups want their _____ _____ settled. _____ _____ want to protect their jobs and communities. _____ _____ do not want unsightly clear cuts where transportation is high. Pulp and paper _____ _____ want a reliable source of wood for their businesses. _____ want to preserve the old-growth forests and watersheds. In order to resolve these various disputes the government has established a _____ to work with the various groups to protect the _____ _____ and the _____.

British Columbia

Worksheet #2: Climate and Industries

Mining:

The _____ in the Western Cordillera contain a wide variety of valuable minerals. _____, _____, _____, asbestos, _____, _____, silver, lead, and molybdenum are minerals mined in British Columbia. The mining industry employs workers such as _____, _____, engineers, heavy equipment workers, and many others.

The mine at _____ produces _____. The smelter at _____ processes aluminum. In the Peace River area, _____ is produced. _____ is mined in the southeast corner of the province. Silver, lead, and zinc are extracted in the _____ _____ area. Copper is the most _____ mineral mined.

Mining is not always a _____ industry, as the need for certain minerals changes. A mining town can suddenly _____ when the material mined is no longer in demand. This has happened in British Columbia when a _____ depends on the mine as the _____ employer.

Energy:

There is an abundance of _____ _____ found in British Columbia. There are _____ coalfields that produce coal which is exported to the _____ _____ countries.

_____ and _____ are piped down the _____ _____ _____ from the Peace River district to Vancouver and the State of Washington in the United States. Other pipelines service other parts of the province.

_____ is made by harnessing the power of four of British Columbia's great rivers, such as the _____, the _____, the _____, and the _____. The _____ built on these rivers supply _____ power to British Columbia.

Tourism:

British Columbia's spectacular _____ and _____ climate on the southern coast attracts visitors the year round. _____ and _____ are popular cities filled with exciting tourist attractions. The _____ and their resorts attract downhill skiers, cross-country skiers, mountain bikers, and snowboarders from all over the world in the _____. In the summer _____, tennis players, hikers, and _____ enjoy the area. The wide variety of _____ attracts many tourists.

British Columbia

Worksheet #2: Climate and Industries

Fishing:

Fishing in British Columbia is big _____. This industry has supported people for _____ of years. The fishing and acquaculture industries harvest more than _____ species of _____ and _____ animals. Along the coast, many _____ plants are located, as well as numerous _____ farms that raise _____ or _____. Thousands of boats are used in the fishing _____.

People employed in the fishing industry are fishing boat _____, marine _____, processing plant _____, and fish _____. Two important fishing centres are _____ in the north and _____ in the south.

British Columbia's waters are fished for salmon, such as _____, _____, _____, _____ and _____. Salmon is _____ prized around the world, whether it is _____, _____, or _____. It makes up more than _____ of the province's ocean _____.

_____ is also fished for its _____ or _____. Tonnes of herring are caught each _____. The roe is removed from the mature _____ fish and exported to _____. The _____ of the herrings are processed for _____ and _____.

The fishing industry in British Columbia has many groups concerned about the _____ fish population. It is felt that this situation has been caused by _____ fishers, _____ fishers, and _____ fishers.

Fishing

Lumbering

Panning for Gold

British Columbia

Worksheet #3: British Columbia's Cities

1. Vancouver

_____ is British Columbia's _____ city and the _____
port in Canada. Its _____ _____ in Burrard Inlet never _____
and allows ships to use it _____. The port handles nearly all of Canada's trade with
_____ and other _____ countries. Vancouver is often called
_____.

    Vancouver has a _____ setting, as it is located near the _____ _____
and the _____ _____. Its _____ is mild, as the city is protected
by the _____ and it receives _____ _____ blowing in from the Pacific
Ocean. Its _____ and _____ make it a very inviting place to live. Its thriving
_____, _____, and _____ communities make it a strong
_____ _____ city.

2. Victoria

    Victoria is the _____ _____ of British Columbia. It is located at the
_____ tip of _____ _____. It is called _____
_____ due to the _____ climate that allows flowers to
bloom _____. _____ _____, located near Victoria, is one of
Canada's most _____ gardens. Many of Victoria's buildings are _____
and _____ and remind tourists of buildings in England. The _____
Hotel is an outstanding, elegant tourist attraction. _____ _____ can be
found in the Royal British Columbia Museum and Thunderbird Park.

3. Mapping Activity:
    On the map of British Columbia, locate and name the following cities. The capital city is marked
with a star inside a circle.

Vancouver	New Westminister	Victoria	Powell River	Duncan
Nanaimo	Prince Rupert	Kamloops	Port Alberni	Kitimat
Penticton	Prince George	Kelowna	Dawson Creek	

| Hell's Gate | Stanley Park | Gas Clock | Capilano Bridge | Rocky Mountains |

SSJ192 ISBN 9781771586900

Map of British Columbia's Cities

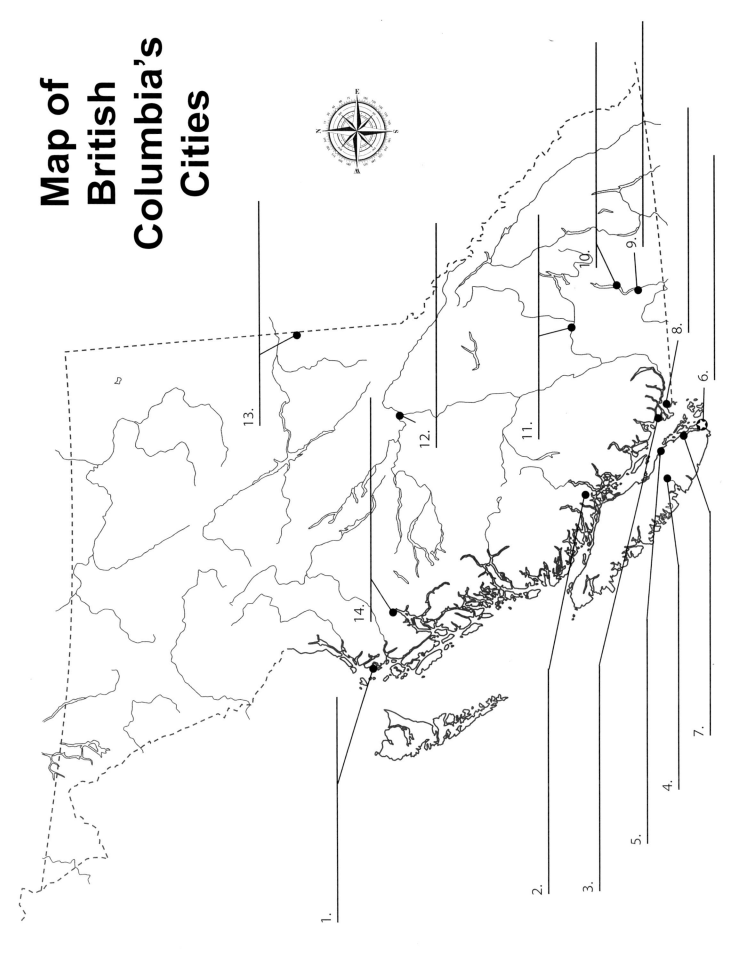

SSJ192   ISBN 9781771586900

British Columbia

Information Sheet

British Columbia's Waterways

British Columbia's landscape is made up of thousands of lakes, rivers, and streams. Most of the large lakes, such as the Okanagan Lake in the south and the Babine Lake in the north, are long and narrow. The lakes lie in valleys formed by the mountains and plateaus. The Okanagan and the Shuswap are lakes found in the south and are used by tourists and campers. Lake Williston and Lake Nechako are water reservoirs created by damming rivers for hydro-electricity. They are the largest man-made lakes in the province. The largest natural lake is Babine Lake.

British Columbia's rivers flow in a north-south direction for most of their route, following the valleys between the mountain ranges. The main rivers of British Columbia drain into the Pacific Ocean. They are the Fraser, Skeena, and the Stikine, which are also important salmon rivers. The Fraser River is British Columbia's major river because it drains about one-quarter of the total area of the province. It begins as a tiny trickle in the Rockies, gathering silt and debris along its way, while growing into a huge waterway that is 1 280 kilometres in length. This massive river has cut a deep, spectacular canyon into the Interior Plateau. At a spot called Hell's Gate, the river rushes through walls 1 000 metres high.

The Nechako, Quesnel, Chilcotin, and Thompson Rivers flow into the Fraser. The Laird and Peace Rivers flow eastward and are part of the Mackenzie River System, which empties into the Arctic Ocean. The Columbia River, the second longest river in North America, is 1 995 kilometres long and drains areas in Canada and the United States. Its water is used for generating hydro-electric power and for irrigation. The Kootenay River is the chief tributary of the Columbia River in British Columbia.

Many waterfalls are found in the mountains of British Columbia. The Della Falls on Vancouver Island is 440 metres high. Near the Bella Coola River in the Coast Mountains is Hulen Falls, which is 274 metres high. In the Yoho Valley of the Rockies is the Takakkaw Falls, which stands 254 metres high.

British Columbia

Worksheet #4: British Columbia's Waterways

Activities:

1. Read the information on "British Columbia's Waterways."

2. Record true or false after the following statements.

    a) The rivers of British Columbia are different from those of the other provinces because they are more turbulent and flow faster. _____

    b) The Fraser is the longest river in Canada. _____

    c) The Columbia River is entirely in British Columbia. _____

    d) Salmon are caught in the Fraser River. _____

    e) The Skeena River empties into the Pacific Ocean. _____

    f) The Okanagan is the largest natural lake in British Columbia. _____

    g) The Fraser River is the longest river in British Columbia. _____

    h) Lake Williston and Lake Nechako are large man-made lakes. _____

    i) The Takakkaw Falls in the Yoho Valley are the highest falls in British Columbia. _____

    j) The Laird River and the Peace River flow into the Columbia River. _____

Mapping Skills:

On the map of British Columbia's Waterways, locate and label the following rivers and lakes.

a) **Rivers:**

    Strikine River; Laird River; Nass River; Skeena River; Thompson River; Fraser River, Columbia River; Okanagan River; Chilcotin River

b) **Lakes:**

    Williston Lake; Babine Lake; Shuswap Lake; Okanagan Lake; Kootenay Lake; Quesnel Lake

c) **Other:**

    Pacific Ocean; Strait of Georgia; Queen Charlotte Strait; Jaun de Fuca Strait; Hecate Strait; Queen Charlotte Islands; Vancouver Island

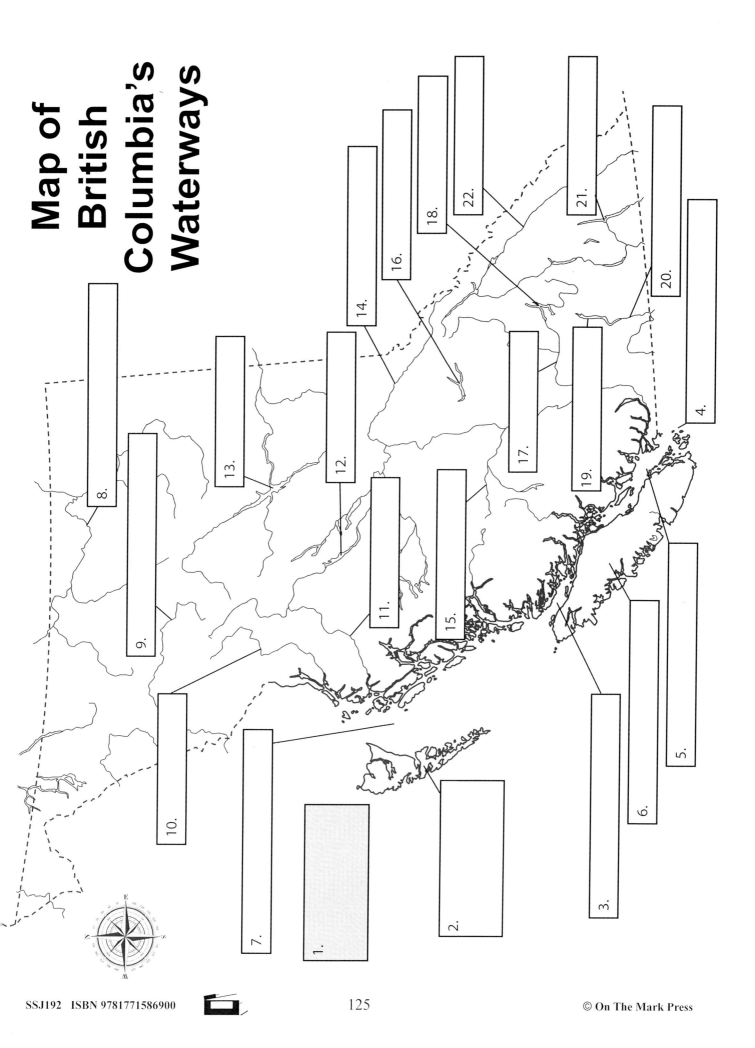

Map of British Columbia's Waterways

SSJ192 ISBN 9781771586900

The Territories

Lesson Plan #17: The Territories

Expectations:

Students will:
- become more knowledgeable and better acquainted with the location, physical features, climate, bodies of water, boundaries, agriculture, mineral resources, industries, cities, symbols, and flags of the Territories of the Yukon, Northwest Territories, and Nunavut.
- develop reading and research skills to locate answers requested.
- identify and label maps of the Yukon, Northwest Territories, and Nunavut.

A. Reproduce the information sheets called "The Territories" found on pages 130, 135, and 140 for your students to read independently or display them on a white board for large group reading and discussion.

Brainstorm and record on three different charts, labelled "The Yukon, "The Northwest Territories," and "Nunavut" for facts the students know about each one. On another chart, list the questions students would like answered about the three territories.

Have your students read the information in each paragraph(s) silently or have a student read it aloud. Then have them locate answers to the following questions.

Information Sheet #1: The Yukon page 130

Paragraph #1: Where are the territories in Canada located? (*northernmost part of Canada*) What are their names? (*Yukon; Northwest Territories; Nunavut*) Have students locate the three territories on a large wall map. How much of Canada do the territories occupy? (*one third of Canada's land mass*)

Paragraphs #2 to #6: Have your students read the secton called "The Yukon." What shape is the Yukon? (*pie-shaped*) What are its boundaries? (*east - Northwest Territories; west - Alaska; south - British Columbia; north - Beaufort Sea*) What are the names of the different types of physical features found in the Yukon? (*glaciers, ice fields, mountains, plateaus, valleys*) What is the name of the mountainous terrain that stretches along the edge of North and South America? (*Cordillera*) What is the name of the second longest river in Canada that flows through the Yukon? (*the Yukon River*) What is the longest river in Canada? (*Mackenzie River*) What other rivers feed the Yukon River? (*Porcupine River, Klondike River, Pelly River*) Why is the Yukon not known for its farmland? (*ground is frozen year round along the Arctic Coast; permafrost*) Describe The Yukon's climate. (*long, cold winters; some areas in the north do not have sunshine; winter lasts from September to June; summers are warm; sun never sets from the end of May to the middle of July; very little rain or snow; air is quite dry*) What is the name of the capital city of the Yukon? (*Whitehorse*) Describe the types of work people in the Yukon do. (*mining; government jobs; guides; some farming; ranching that raises elk, bison, reindeer, musk oxen for meat and hides; Aboriginal art*)

The Territories

Information Sheet #2: The Northwest Territories page 135

Paragraph #1 to 6: What are the borders of the Northwest Territories? (*Yukon to the west; Nunavut to the east; Arctic Ocean to the north; British Columbia, Alberta and Saskatchewan to the south*) What are the two main physical features in the Northwest Territories? (*Canadian Shield; Interior Plains*) What do you find in the Northwest Territories? (*mountains; winding rivers; deep valleys; rushing waterfalls; pine forests*) Where do the trees not grow in the Northwest Territories? (*above the treeline*) What is the name of Canada's longest river that flows through this territory? (*Mackenzie River*) Where do most of the people live in the Northwest Territories? (*the Mackenzie Valley*) What is the name of the capital city? (*Yellowknife*) Why does nothing grow near the Arctic Ocean? (*land is rocky; permanently frozen; permafrost; tundra*) Describe the climate of the Northwest Territories. (*dry; very little snow or rain; winters extremely cold in the north; warmer in the Mackenzie Valley*) At what do the people in the Northwest Territories work? (*seasonal work; hunt and fish for food; trap animals for their furs; work as guides; do handicrafts; some mine; work at oil wells; government jobs*)

Information Sheet #3: Nunavut Territory page 140

Paragraph #1: When did Nunavut become a territory? (*April 1, 1999*) What does its name mean? (*"our land"*)

Paragraph #2: Where is Nunavut located? (*east of the Northwest Territories; north of Manitoba*) What does Nunavut have more of than the other provinces and territories in Canada? (*more land area; longest coastline*) What is the shape of Nunavut? (*shaped something like an inukshuk or a pile of stones stacked to look like a human*) What is Nunavut's main physical feature? (*Canadian Shield*) What are the names of the two main land regions in Nunavut? (*Arctic Mainland; Arctic Islands*) Describe the land in Nunavut. (*rocky, swampy, permafrost*)

Paragraph #3: Describe the communities found in Nunavut. (*small, few in number; spread far apart*) What is the name of Nunavut's capital city? (*Iqaluit*) Who mainly lives in Nunavut? (*Inuit*)

Paragraph #4: What is the climate like in Nunavut? (*coldest weather in Canada; low temperatures; freezing winds; icy blizzards; blowing snow; some places located near the North Pole have sunlight all day and night during the summer; during winter it is the opposite; there is no light of any kind for days; receives very little snow or rain*

Paragraph #5: How do the people in Nunavut travel from place to place? (*travel by air, boats, all-terrain vehicles, snowmobiles, dog sleds*) Why? (*There are no roads or highways*)

Paragraph #6: What types of jobs do the people in Nunavut work at? (*guides, construction, government jobs, artisans, service jobs such as teachers, nurses, doctors, electricians*) Why do you think the Inuit children are taught traditional ways and values by the elders of a community? (*so they can pass the traditions on to their children; to make them proud of their heritage*)

Answer Key for Worksheets #1 – #3 The Yukon Territory pages 131 to 133
Location: *northwestern; triangular; Alaska; Northwest Territories; British Columbia; Beaufort Sea*

The Territories

Land Surface: *mountains; plains; plateaus; valleys; Western Cordillera; Interior Plateau; Eastern Cordillera; Arctic Coastal Plain; Saint Elias; Coast; tallest; Mount Logan; highest; Canada; North America; 5 959; Glaciers; ice fields*

Territorial Climate: *Subarctic; - 40°C; 30°C; long; dark; freeze; middle; December; no; three; five; dry climate; light; snow; ploughed; pleasant; short; longest; 24 hours; 21 hours; 19 hours; twilight; Land of the Midnight Sun*

Industries:

Mining: *backbone; gold; Klondike; Gold; ten; Lead; zinc; ore; mined out; world; low*

Tourism: *second; wilderness; history; adventures; tours; canoeing; rafting; employs; quarter*

The Government: *government; highest; federal; territorial; municipal*

The Fur Trade: *trapping; trading; Hudson Bay Company; some; uncertain; fluctuate; demand; decreased; Beavers; martens; lynxes; foxes; minks*

Forestry: *slowly; fifty; Forest fires; lightning; not; three; Watson Lake; Whitehorse*

Farming: *poor; rainfall; permafrost; long; sunlight; quickly; important; successful; vegetables; field crops; Whitehorse; commercial; vegetables; seeds; pigs; chickens; goats; reindeer; Pelly; crops; cattle*

Fishing: *important; chinook; chum; sold; Trout; Arctic char; Sport; dollars; Anglers; waters*

The Yukon's Cities and Towns:

1. *Whitehorse; west; Yukon; modern; log cabins; log-scrapers; S.S. Klondyke; sternwheelers*
2. *Dawson City; Yukon; Klondike; wide; boardwalks; Robert Service's; houses; stores; hotels*

Answer Key for Map of the Yukon Territory page 134

1. *Old Crow* 2. *Dawson City* 3. *Carmacks* 4. *Haines Junction* 5. *Faro* 6. *Whitehorse*
7. *Carcross* 8. *Teslin* 9. *Watson Lake*

Answer Key for Worksheet #1: The Northwest Territories page 136

Location: *middle; Yukon; Nunavut; Beaufort Sea; British Columbia; Alberta; Saskatchewan*

Land Surface: *wilderness; mountains; valleys; forests; ice-capped; three; Arctic Mainland; Mackenzie Valley; Arctic Islands; Canadian Shield; horseshoe; bedrock; minerals*

Territorial Climate: *not; snow; ice; less; southern; blown; winds; rains; desert; warm; hot; 21°C; 40°C; cold; winds; long; Arctic; nine; celebrate; brighter; warmer; longer; short; quickly; long; hours*

The Northwest Territories' Worksheet #2 Page 137

Mining: *mineral; important; development; expensive; extract; transport; government; most; important; more money*

Oil and Gas: *offshore; oil; onshore; gas; active; Bent Horn; Pointed Mountain; Norman Wells; artificial islands; pipeline*

Trapping and Hunting:

oldest; most important; *changes; trapping; killing; beaver; fox; lynx; marten; mink; muskrat; wolf; caribou; moose; musk-ox; seal; whale; grouse; ptarmigan; duck; goose; harvested; exported; Sports hunting; hunters; big game; polar bear hunt; $17 000; Inuit; good*

Fishing: *lakes; streams; commercial; tourists; sport; release; stocks; lodges; Great Bear Lake; Great Slave Lake; commercial*

The Territories

Answer Key for Worksheet #3: The Northwest Territories page 138
Forestry: *not; limited; treeline; useful; sawmills; shortage; lack; knowledgeable*
Farming: *farms; Hay River; chicken; egg; cattle; bison; market garden; Fort Simpson; Fort Smith; Tuktoyaktuk; reindeer; meat; antlers; Hydroponic; greenhouses; community*

The Northwest Territories' Cities and Towns:
1. *Yellowknife; Great Slave Lake; gateway; streets; skyscrapers; modern; prospectors'; quonset; makeshift; prospectors; Ingraham Trail; Great Slave Lake; Mackenzie River;* 2. *Fort Smith; second; national; Wood Buffalo National Park; Rafters; rapids; portage; route* 3. *Inuvik; largest; north; modern; Aklavik; Delta*

Map of the Northwest Territory: Cities and Towns page 139
1. *Tuktayaktuk* 2. *Inuvik* 3. *Norman Wells* 4. *Deline* 5. *Fort Norman* 6. *Wrigley* 7. *Fort Simpson*
8. *Rae* 9. *Yellowknife* 10. *Fort Resolution* 11. *Pine Point* 12. *Fort Smith* 13. *Hay River*
14. *Fort Laird*

Answer Key for Worksheet #1: Nunavut Territory page 141
Location: *Northwest Territories; Inuit; west; Greenland; Manitoba; Arctic Ocean*
Land Surface: *coastline; larger; above the treeline; no trees grow; Canadian Shield*
Territorial Climate: *coldest; nine; -30°C; blizzards; blowing; colder; warm; 30°C; summer; towards; closest; continual; sunlight; midnight; opposite; away; northernmost; constant darkness*
Industries: *remote; transportation; slow; expensive; industries; economy*
The Inuit Lifestyle: *variety; construction; tour guides; artisans; tapestries; carvings; sculptures*

Answer Key for Worksheet #2: Nunavut Territory page 142
Government Jobs: *government; doctors; nurses*
Tourism: *fastest; work; outfitters; rents; tents; kayaks; explore; guides; paddle; kayak; hiking; climb*
Construction: *expanding; rapidly; busy; schools; offices; community; homes*
Mining: *rich deposits; lead; zinc; Little Cornwallis Island; Arctic Bay; Lupin Mine; Contwoyto Lake; gold; Oil; gas; Bent Horn; Cameron Island*
Manufacturing: *factories; processing; meat; fish; build; create*

Answer Key for Worksheet #3: Nunavut Territory page 143
Nunavut's Cities and Towns:
Paragraph1. *small; few; far; 22 000; isolated; Iqaluit; largest; capital city; Baffin;*
Paragraph 2: *Toonik Tyme; Pond Inlet; history; modern*
Paragraph 3: *permanently; buildings; completely; pipes; water; fuel; above*

Map of the Communities in Nunavut page 144
1. *Resolute* 2. *Pond Inlet* 3. *Pangnirtung* 4. *Iqaluit* 5. *Cape Dorset* 6. *Arviat* 7. *Whale Cove*
8. *Rankin Inlet* 9. *Chesterfield Inlet* 10. *Baker Lake* 11. *Repulse Bay* 12. *Gjoa Haven*
13. *Kugluktuk* 14. *Cambridge Bay* 15. *Alert*

The Territories

Information Sheet

The Territories make up more than one third of Canada's land mass. They are located in the northern part of Canada. There are three territories: the Yukon Territory, the Northwest Territories, and Nunavut.

The Yukon

The Yukon is a pie-shaped wedge located in the northwestern corner of Canada. It is squeezed between the Northwest Territories on the east, Alaska on the west, and British Columbia to the south, while the icy waters of the Beaufort Sea form the Yukon's northern coastline.

Many long chains of rugged mountains divided by plateaus and deep valleys are found throughout the territory. These land forms are a part of the Cordillera, a belt of mountainous terrain, that stretches along the entire edge of North and South America. Many glaciers and ice fields are found in the mountains. The mighty Yukon River, the second longest river in Canada, flows through this territory. It is fed by other large rivers such as the Porcupine, the Klondike, and the Pelly. In the northernmost areas along the Arctic Coast, the ground remains frozen year round, and is called *permafrost*.

The Yukon's climate is long and cold during the winter months and some areas near the Arctic Circle do not receive any sunshine. Winter lasts from September to June. In the summer the opposite occurs. From the end of May until the middle of July, the sun nevers sets. Yukon summers are warm and the temperature can vary between10°C to 27°C. Very little rain or snow falls in the Yukon and the air is quite dry.

The population of the Yukon is 33 897 (2011 census) and is made up of a variety of ethnic backgrounds. The capital city of the Yukon is Whitehorse, which has a population of around 22 984.

Gold and other minerals are mined and mining employs about six percent of the people in the Yukon. Many other people in the Yukon are employed by the government. Some people work as guides for sport fishermen and hunters or take people rafting on many of the scenic rivers during the summer. Some farming and ranching is also done. Elk, bison, reindeer, and musk oxen are raised for their meat and hides. Many of the Aboriginal peoples create beautiful art pieces for tourists to buy or they sell them elsewhere.

Symbols of the Yukon Territory

The Yukon's Flag

Fireweed

The Territories

Worksheet #1: The Yukon Territory

Location:

The Yukon Territory is located in the extreme _____ part of Canada. It is _____ in shape. To the west it borders the state of _____ and to the east it borders the _____. The Yukon's southern border is the province of _____ and to the north it borders the salt waters of the _____.

Land Surface:

The Yukon Territory is an area filled with _____, _____ and _____ separated by _____. The Yukon is divided into four main regions. They are the _____, the _____, the _____, and the _____. The _____ Range and the _____Mountains cover the southwestern corner of the Yukon. Some of the _____ peaks in North America are found in these mountains. _____, a massive mountain, is found in the Saint Elias Range, and it is the _____ in _____ and the second highest in _____.It is _____ metres high. _____ and permanent _____ are also found in the Saint Elias Mountains.

Territorial Climate:

The Yukon Territory is located in the _____ climate zone. Its temperatures can range from _____ or colder to _____ or warmer. Winters are _____ and _____. Lakes and rivers begin to _____ by early October. By the _____ of _____, some places receive _____ daylight, while other places may receive _____ to _____ hours of daylight.

The Yukon Territory has a _____ and receives _____ snowfalls. There is so little _____ that the main roads do not get _____.

Yukon summers are _____ but _____. Temperatures usually reach the mid-twenties. The middle of summer falls on June 21, which is the _____ day of the season and year. Places like Old Crow experience _____ of sun. Dawson City receives _____ and Whitehorse and Watson get _____. Throughout the territory, the _____ lasts almost until sunrise. The Yukon is often referred to as the " _____ " for this reason.

Northern Lights   **Miles Canyon**   **Dawson City**

SSJ192   ISBN 9781771586900

The Territories

Worksheet #2: The Yukon Territory

Industries:

The Canadian Government heavily subsidizes the Yukon Territory due to its remoteness and small population. Without this help, the Yukon could not keep up to its present standard.

Mining

Mining has been the _____ of the Yukon's economy ever since _____ was discovered in the _____ a hundred years ago. _____ mining accounts for _____ percent of the Yukon's mineral production. _____ and _____ are now the territory's most important minerals. Many of the large mines have closed down because the _____ was_____ _____ or because the _____ metal prices were too _____ to carry on with mining operations.

Tourism

Tourism is the Yukon's _____ largest industry. Travellers come from all over the world to view its _____ beauty and to learn about its _____. Tourists come to participate in wilderness _____, _____, _____ and river_____. Tourism _____ almost a _____ of the territory's non-government workforce.

The Government

The _____ employs the _____ number of people in the territory. They perform a wide range of jobs for the _____, _____, and _____ governments.

The Fur Trade

Fur _____ and _____ is the Yukon's oldest industry. It dates back in time to when the _____ first began to explore the territory. Trapping today does provide a living for _____ Yukoners but it is an _____ occupation. Fur prices often _____ and the _____ for fur coats and fur clothing has _____ in recent years. _____, _____, _____, _____, and _____ are the popular animals that are trapped for their furs.

Forestry

Trees grow very _____ in the Yukon and take _____ years to mature. _____ _____started by _____ strikes destroy millions of hectares of trees every year. Forestry is _____ an important industry in the Yukon. There are _____ mills near _____ in southeastern Yukon. Several small sawmills operate near _____.

The Territories

Worksheet #3: The Yukon Territory

Farming

Farming areas are limited in the Yukon due to _____ soil, low _____, and _____. In good areas where farming is successful, the _____ hours of _____ help the plants to grow _____.

Although farming is not an _____ industry, there are a number of _____ farming operations. Near Dawson, where the soil has been made fertile by the flooding of rivers, _____ and certain _____ grow successfully. In the _____ area there are a small number of family-run _____ farms. They produce products such as _____, _____, _____, rabbits, _____, sheep, _____, fish, and _____. A farm on the _____ River successfully raises _____ and _____.

Fishing

Fishing is more _____ to the Yukon economy than farming. At Dawson, _____ and _____ salmon are caught in the rivers and then processed. These fish are _____ to Germany, Japan, and other countries. _____ is plentiful and sold commercially. _____, a northern delicacy, is sold to restaurants all over the world. _____ fishing brings in many _____ to the Yukon. _____ from all over the world love to fish in the Yukon's sparkling, cold, clear _____ found in its lakes and streams.

The Yukon's Cities and Towns

1. _____ is the capital city of the Yukon Territory. It lies on the _____ bank of the _____ River. Large _____ homes can be seen standing with older _____ _____, still in use on the streets. One major tourist attraction is the two-and-three storey _____. Tourists love to tour the _____, the largest and last of the _____ that travelled the Yukon River.

2. _____ is famous for its Klondike Gold Rush days. It lies at the junction of the _____ and the _____ Rivers. Every year, tourists come to wander the town's _____ streets and wooden _____ and then stop at _____ log cabin to hear actors reading his poetry. Dawson City's streets are lined with brightly painted _____, _____, and _____ that look the same as they did during the gold rush days.

3. **Mapping Activity:** On a map of the Yukon, locate and label the important centres listed below. The capital city is located at the star inside a circle. Print the names neatly on the lines.

> Teslin   Watson Lake   Whitehorse   Dawson City   Faro
> Old Crow   Haines Junction   Carcross   Carmacks

Cities and Towns of the Yukon Territory

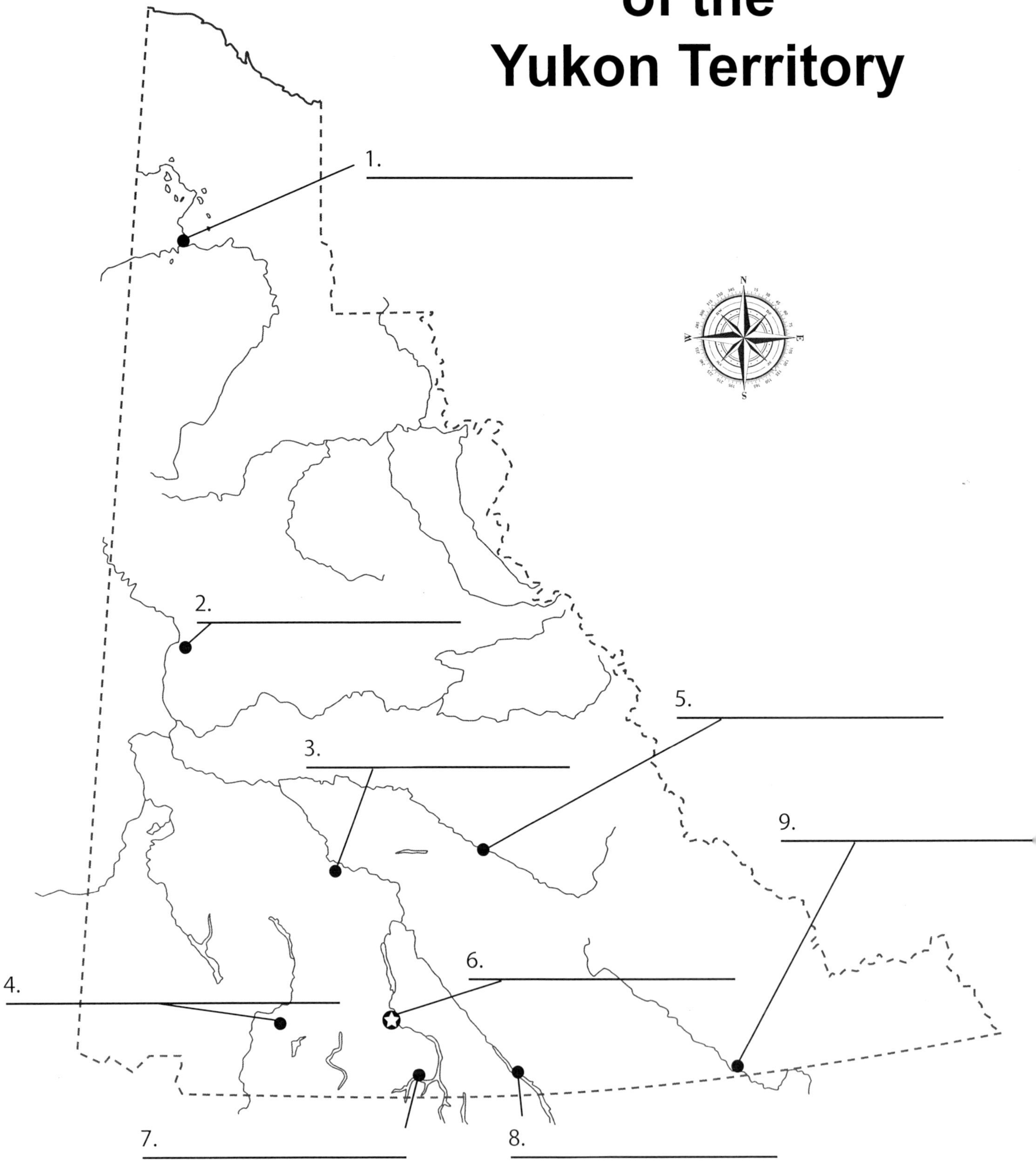

1. _____

2. _____

3. _____

4. _____

5. _____

6. _____

7. _____

8. _____

9. _____

SSJ192 ISBN 9781771586900

The Territories

Information Sheet

The Northwest Territories

The Northwest Territories is a large area of land located between the Yukon to the west, Nunavut to the east, the Arctic Ocean to the north, and British Columbia, Alberta, and Saskatchewan to the south.

The Canadian Shield and the Interior Plains are the two main physical regions in this territory. Most of the Northwest Territories lies above the tree line. The Northwest Territories are filled with majestic mountains, winding rivers, deep valleys, rushing waterfalls, and pine forests.

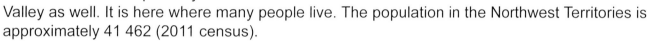

The Mackenzie River is the longest river in Canada and empties into the Arctic Ocean. It flows through the Mackenzie Valley, where most of the people in the territories live. Yellowknife is the capital city and is found in the Mackenzie Valley as well. It is here where many people live. The population in the Northwest Territories is approximately 41 462 (2011 census).

The land near the Arctic Ocean is rocky and treeless tundra. The permanently frozen ground of the tundra is called *permafrost*.

The Northwest Territories experiences a dry climate. It receives very little snow or rain throughout the year. Winters are extremely cold, with temperatures about -32°C. Temperatures in the Mackenzie Valley can be warmer. In the summer, temperatures may hover around 21°C.

The people who live in the Northwest Territories must be very versatile, as the work is seasonal. Many Aboriginal People hunt and fish for food and trap animals for their furs. Some take tourists on guided tours, camping trips, and fishing expeditions through the land. Handicrafts are made to sell to the tourists, and they are also sold to other markets. Some mining of gold is done at Yellowknife. Oil is produced at Norman Wells. Many people are employed by the government and perform important service jobs.

Symbols for the Northwest Territories

Flag of the Northwest Territories

White Mountain Avens

The Territories

Worksheet #1: The Northwest Territories

Location:

The Northwest Territories is located in the _____ of Canada's other northern territories. To the west it borders the _____, and to the east it borders _____. To the north it borders the _____ _____, and to the south it borders the provinces of _____, _____, and _____.

Land Surface:

The Northwest Territories is one of North America's last _____ regions. It is filled with majestic _____, deep _____, pine _____ and some _____ islands. It has _____ main physical regions. They are the _____, the _____, and the _____. The Northwest Territories is covered mainly by the _____ which is a huge_____ of solid _____ that is two to four billion years old. This bedrock is the storage place for many of Canada's _____.

Climate:

The Northwest Territories is _____ covered with _____ and _____ all year long. It receives _____ than many places in _____ Canada. Snow does fall, but it gets _____ away by howling _____. It seldom _____ in the Northwest Territories. Some scientists classify it as a _____ because it is so dry.

Summers can be quite _____and sometimes even _____. Summer temperatures often hover around _____. July temperatures in Fort Smith have been recorded as high as _____.

Winters are very _____ with harsh _____, and they are very _____. Winter in the _____ areas lasts for at least _____ months.

In the spring, snow and ice still cover the ground, but the people _____ the arrival of spring. It is still cold, but the sunlight is _____ and appears _____. The days are _____. Summer is _____, but the plants grow _____ due to the _____ _____ of daylight.

Inuvik on the Mackenzie River

Sambass Heh Falls

Ferry Boat on Laird River

The Territories

Worksheet #2: Northwest Territories

Industries:

Mining

The Northwest Territories is known to have almost every _____ that has been discovered. These minerals will play an _____ role in the _____ of the Northwest Territories. At the present time it is very _____ to _____ the minerals and to _____ them to other countries. The _____ has very ambitious plans for overcoming these obstacles. Mining is the _____ _____ industry and brings in _____ _____ than any other industry.

Oil and Gas

In the Northwest Territories, _____ areas seem rich in _____, while _____ areas are richer in _____. There are three _____ oil and gas fields in the Northwest Territories. They are located at _____ in the Arctic Islands, _____ near Fort Laird, and _____ on the Mackenzie River. The Norman Wells oil field has been the most successful. Six _____ _____ were constructed in the Mackenzie River in 1982, and a _____ from Norman Wells to Zama, Alberta was built in 1985 to link up with other pipelines.

Trapping and Hunting

The fur trade is the _____ industry in the Northwest Territories and once was the _____ _____. The _____ in fashion and the people who are against the _____ and _____ of animals for their fur have weakened this industry. The animals mainly caught are _____, arctic red _____, _____, _____, _____, _____, and _____.

Many animals such as _____, _____, _____, _____, _____, and various birds such as _____, _____, _____ and _____ are hunted and eaten by small communities. Wild game is _____ and _____ to other places.

_____ _____ is an important industry, as _____ come from around the world to hunt _____ _____ such as polar bear, musk-ox, caribou, moose, and grizzly bear. The _____ is considered the ultimate adventure for a hunter. Each hunter may pay up to _____ for a hunt. The _____ can earn _____ money by providing the service.

Fishing

The people in the Northwest Territories have fished the _____ and _____ for food for many years. Today, fishing is also a _____ industry. Many _____ come to fish for _____ and are asked to _____ any fish they catch. This helps to protect the _____ of fish. Fishing _____ are open from June to September. _____ and _____ are popular fishing spots. Great Slave Lake also has a _____ whitefish fishery.

The Territories

Worksheet #3: Northwest Territories

Forestry:

Forestry is _____ a big industry in the Northwest Territories because it is _____ to areas south of the _____. There is a large area of _____ forest, but there are very few _____. The forest industry has not grown due to the _____ of roads, and the _____ of money and _____ people.

Farming

The Northwest Territories does have some _____, but they are not like the ones that we see in the rest of Canada. Most of the farms are found near _____. Here you will find a _____farm, an _____ production farm, a _____ ranch, a _____ ranch, and a large _____ _____. Near_____ _____ there is more market gardening. _____ _____ has a small cattle ranch, and near _____, a herd of _____ provides _____and _____ for a small market. _____ gardening, _____, and local _____ gardens help to provide fresh vegetables.

The Northwest Territories' Cities and Towns

1. _____ is the capital city of the Northwest Territories. It is located on the north shore of _____. Yellowknife is considered the _____ to the entire territory. Yellowknife's _____ have a mixture of large _____, _____ houses, _____ shacks, and _____ huts, which were _____ homes left by the early _____. Tourists enjoy driving the _____, sailing on _____ or cruising the _____.

2. _____ is known as the Garden Capital of the North. The _____ largest _____ park in the world is found near Fort Smith. It is called _____ _____. _____ come here to travel through the historic _____ and _____ the _____ on the Slave River.

3. _____ is the _____ Canadian Community _____ of the Arctic Circle. It was the first _____ town built by the government to replace _____, which appeared to be sinking into the _____.

4. **Mapping Activity:** On a map of the Northwest Territories, label the following cities and towns. The capital city is marked with a star inside a circle. Print the names neatly on the lines.

Tuktoyaktuk	**Inuvik**	**Yellowknife**	**Fort Simpson**	**Fort Smith**
Fort Resolution	**Rae**	**Fort Norman**	**Hay River**	**Pine Point**
Norman Wells	**Wrigley**	**Fort Laird**	**Deline**	

SSJ192 ISBN 9781771586900

Cities and Towns of The Northwest Territories

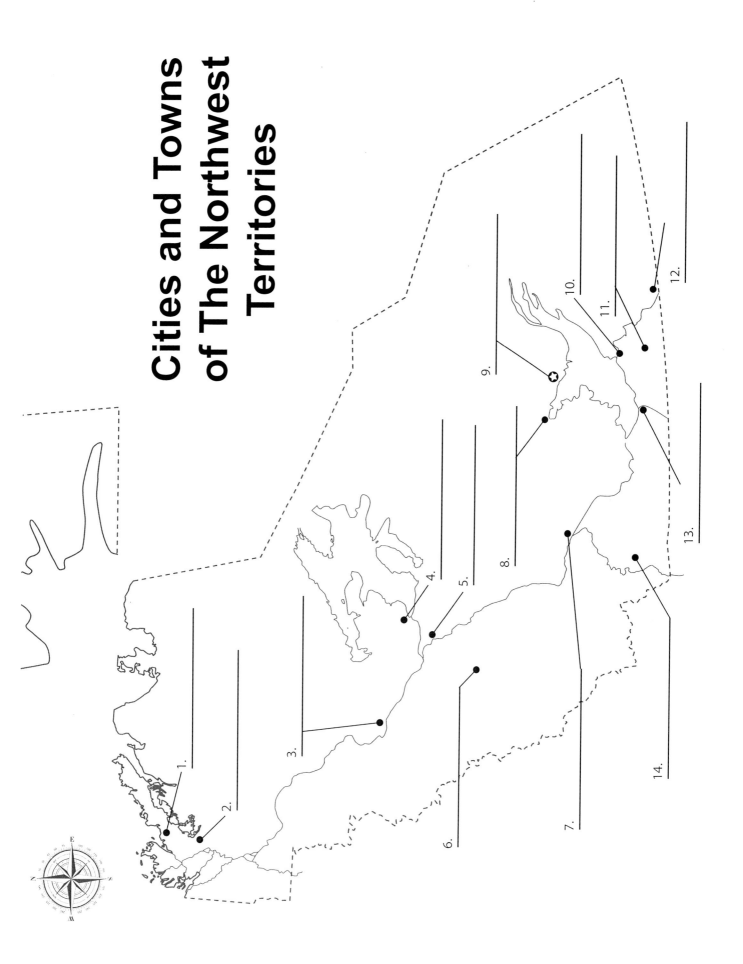

SSJ192   ISBN 9781771586900

The Territories

Information Sheet

Nunavut Territory

Nunavut is a newly-formed territory that was carved out of the Northwest Territories on April 1, 1999. It was officially declared a Canadian territory with its own government and judicial court. Nunavut means "our land" in Inuktituk.

Nunavut is located east of the Northwest Territories and north of Manitoba. It has a greater land area than any other province or territory and the longest coastline in Canada. Nunavut is shaped somewhat like an "inukshuk" or pile of stones stacked to look like a human. Most of Nunavut is made up of the Canadian Shield. It is divided into two main land regions: the Arctic Mainland and the Arctic Islands. Most of the land is rocky, swampy, or permafrost.

The communities are small, few in number, and spread far apart. Large communities are Iqaluit, Rankin Inlet, and Cambridge Bay. Iqaluit is the capital city of this new territory. The total population of Nunavut is approximately 31 906 (2011 census). Mainly Inuit live in this territory.

Nunavut has the coldest weather in Canada. The average temperature is 9°C. In the winter, the temperature can dip to a chilling -30°C. Freezing winds, icy blizzards, and blowing snow make the winters seem even colder. During the summer, places closest to the North Pole in Nunavut have sunlight all day and night as the Earth is tilted towards the sun. In the winter, it is the opposite, and there is no sunlight or light of any kind for days. Nunavut receives very little snow or rain.

Nunavut does not have any highways or roads connecting the communities. The people must travel by airplane, boat, or on an all-terrain vehicle. In the winter, the people use snowmobiles or dog sleds.

Inuit fill a variety of positions within the workforce of Nunavut. They perform an assortment of jobs, which can include guides to tourists, construction workers, and artisans. Inuit are being trained in many service jobs and are the teachers, nurses, doctors, electricians, etc. of this territory. The Inuit elders continue teaching children the traditional ways and values of the Inuit society.

Nunavut's Symbols

Nunavut's Flag

Nunavut's Coat of Arms

Nunavut's Flower-Purple Saxifrage

 # The Territories

Worksheet #1: Nunavut Territory

Location:

Nunavut is a fairly new territory carved out of the _____ for the
_____ people. On the _____, it borders the Northwest Territories, and to
the east across Baffin Bay and Davis Strait lies the country of _____. To the south it
borders _____ and to the north the _____.

Land Surface:

Nunavut has two-thirds of Canada's _____. It is _____ than any
other territory or province in Canada. Its coastline is stretched around many islands, bays,
channels and inlets. Nunavut is located "_____,"
a region of the world where _____. Much of this territory rests on the
hard rock called the _____ _____.

Territorial Climate:

Nunavut has the _____ weather in Canada. Winter lasts about _____
months of the year, and the average temperature is _____. During this season,
_____,and _____ winds are experienced which make the winter appear
even _____.

In the summer, Nunavut can get quite _____. Temperatures have been recorded
as high as _____ in Coppermine, one of Nunavut's coastal communities.

Nunavut is also considered the "Land of the Midnight Sun." During the _____,
the North Pole tilts _____ the sun. Hence the areas of Nunavut that are
_____ to the North Pole have summer days of almost _____
_____, even at _____. In the winter, it is the _____. During
this season, the North Pole tilts _____ from the sun and the _____
areas of Nunavut experience _____ _____.

Industries:

Nunavut is very _____, and _____ is either _____
or _____, therefore very few _____ have developed in the territory. The
_____ of Nunavut is shaped by many factors, which include climate, lifestyle, and
resources.

The Lifestyle of the Inuit:

Inuit work at a _____ of jobs. Some of the jobs they have are as _____
workers and _____. These jobs are seasonal. The Inuit are well-known
_____, making _____, _____, and _____
specific to the Inuit way of life. This art is sold in local communties, as well as exported and sold
in shops across North America.

The Territories

Worksheet #2: Nunavut Territory

Government Jobs

The Inuit have a variety of positions. Some of these are in the service sector running their
_____. They are the _____, _____, electricians, and
teachers of the future. Inuit are striving to be at the cutting edge of developing their own territory.

Tourism

Tourism is the _____ growing part of the territory's economy.
The Inuit _____ at jobs as tour guides, hotel clerks, and cooks. Many work as
_____. An outfitter _____ outdoor equipment, such as _____
and _____ to visitors who come to _____ Nunavut's wilderness.

Hunting and fishing _____ take tourists to good fishing areas. Some help tourists
_____ the wild rivers or _____ amongst the Arctic Islands. Because of
their extensive knowledge of the land, Inuit guides take tourists on _____ trips
across the tundra or help them _____ mountains and glaciers.

Construction

Communties in Nunavut are _____ _____. The construction
business is very _____. New buildings such as _____,
_____, _____ centres, and _____ are being constructed.

Mining

Nunavut has _____ _____ of minerals. Miners dig for
_____ and _____ at the Polaris Mine on _____ _____
_____ or at the Nanisivik mine near _____ _____. The _____
_____ on _____ _____ is the world's northernmost gold
mine. It is one of Canada's top five _____ producers.
_____ and _____ has also been located in Nunavut. There is one small
oil field in production called _____ on _____ _____.

Manufacturing

There are very few _____ in Nunavut. Most workers work at _____
food. Raw _____ and _____ are cut up and packaged. Nunavut plans to
_____ more factories to _____ more jobs.

The Territories

Worksheet #3: Nunavut Territory

The Cities and Towns of Nunavut

1. Many of the communties in Nunavut are _____, _____ in number, and _____ from one another. There are approximately _____ people living in Nunavut. The people are scattered about throughout the territory in 28 _____ communities. _____ is the _____ community, with 3 552 residents. It is the _____ _____ of Nunavut and is located on _____ Island.

2. Every year, there is a spring celebration called _____ held in Iqaluit. In _____ _____, there is Tununiq Theatre, where actors portray both the _____ and _____ Inuit ways.

3. In Nunavut, the ground is _____ frozen. All the _____ are built to sit _____ above ground. Even the _____ carrying _____ and _____ must be _____ ground.

2. **Mapping Activity:** Using a map of Nunavut, locate and label the following communities.

Baker Lake	**Cape Dorset**	**Cambridge Bay**	**Kugluktuk**	**Resolute**
Arviat	**Pond Inlet**	**Rankin Inlet**	**Repulse Bay**	**Whale Cove**
Iqaluit	**Pangnirtung**	**Chesterfield Inlet**	**Gjoa Haven**	**Alert**

Iceberg near Baffin Island

A Way to Travel in Nunavut

Inuit Man Wearing Goggles

Polar Bear on Ice Floe

Inuit Inukshuk on Fiord of Baffin Island

Baird's Sandpiper on Tundra

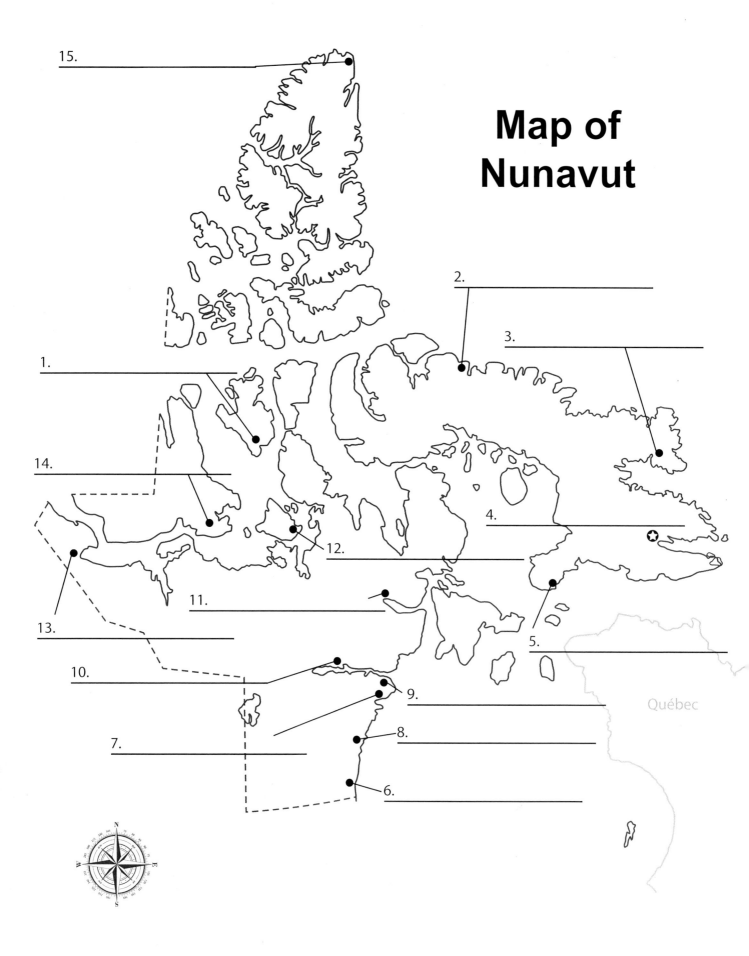

Map of Nunavut

15. _____

2. _____

3. _____

1. _____

14. _____

4. _____

12. _____

11. _____

5. _____

13. _____

10. _____

9. _____

8. _____

7. _____

6. _____

Québec

SSJ192   ISBN 9781771586900